ADVICE REGARDING THE BOOK OF ALLAH

By the Noble Scholar Shaykh Hafidh al-Hakami

Explained By
Shaykh Abdur Razzaq al-Badr

ISBN: 978-1-7923-0836-9

First Edition: Sha'ban 1440 A.H. / April 2019 C.E.

Cover Design: Usul Design
E-mail: info@usuldesign.com

Translator: Rasheed Barbee

Editing & Formatting: Razan Gregory
Annurediting.com

Publisher's Information:

Authentic Statements Publishing
P. O. Box 15536
Philadelphia, PA. 19131
215.382.3382
215.382.3782-Fax

Store:
5000 Locust Street (Side Entrance)
Philadelphia, Pa 19139

Website: www.authenticstatements.com
E-mail: info@authenticstatements.com

Transliteration Table

Consonants

ء	'	د	d	ض	ḍ	ك	k
ب	b	ذ	dh	ط	ṭ	ل	l
ت	t	ر	r	ظ	ẓ	م	m
ث	th	ز	z	ع	ʿ	ن	n
ج	j	س	s	غ	gh	ه	h
ح	ḥ	ش	sh	ف	f	و	w
خ	kh	ص	ṣ	ق	q	ي	y

Vowels

Short	◌َ	a	◌ِ	i	◌ُ	u
Long	ـَا	ā	ـِي	ī	ـُو	ū
Diphthongs	ـَي	ay	ـَو	aw		

Glyphs

ﷺ *Sallallāhu ʿalayhi wa sallam* (May Allāh's praise & salutations be upon him)

ʿAlayhis-salām (Peace be upon him)

ʿAza wa jal (Mighty and Majestic)

Radiyallāhu ʿanhu (May Allāh be pleased with him)

Radiyallāhu ʿanha (May Allāh be pleased with her)

Rahimahullah (May Allāh have mercy upon him)

Table of Contents

Biography of Shaykh Ḥāfidh ibn Aḥmad ibn ʿAlī al-Ḥakami

Shaykh Hāfidh ibn Aḥmad ibn 'Alī Al-Ḥakami ﷺ was one of the Salafi scholars from the Kingdom of Saudi Arabia. He is one of the flag-bearers of knowledge from the southern region of the country known as Tihamah, during the 14th century after the migration. The name al-Ḥakami is an ascription to al-Ḥakm ibn Sa'd al Ashīra, who are descendents from the Madḥaj tribe.

His birth and upbringing:

Shaykh Ḥāfidh was born on the 24th night of Ramadan, during the year 1342H, which coincides with the year 1924 C.E., in a coastal village called as-Salām, just outside the city of Jāzān. He was raised under the care of his two parents. He received a good upbringing and he was cultivated upon chastity, purity and good character. Before the age of puberty, he worked as a shepherd, herding the sheep of his parents. This was the most important wealth of the society during those days. However, Ḥāfidh was not like the other young boys in the community.

Indeed, he was special with regard to his intelligence, memory and understanding. He memorized the Qur'an before the age of 12. He, likewise, learned proficiency in handwriting while young.

His Religious Studies:

During the year 1358H, which coincides with the year 1940 C.E., the grand Mufti of Saudi Arabia, Shaykh Muḥammad Ibrahīm 'Āli Shaykh sent Shaykh 'Abdullah al-Qur'āwī to the city of Tihamah to teach the people and remove ignorance. Shaykh Ḥāfidh, and his older brother Muḥammad, went to Shaykh Al-Qur'āwī with a letter requesting some books on *tawhīd* and expressing their regret at being unable to study with him because they were busy serving and seeing to their parents' needs. They requested the Shaykh visit their village so that they might benefit from some of his lessons. He accepted their invitation and went to their village, where he met the young Ḥāfidh and got to know him very well; and saw in him promising signs of excellence and intelligence.

When Shaykh al-Qur'āwī was ready to return to the city of Sāmitah, he asked the parents of Shaykh Ḥāfidh to permit him to employ someone to herd their sheep on his behalf, in exchange for their permission that Shaykh Hāfidh and his older brother return with him to Sāmitah so that they might seek knowledge there underneath his care. Initially their parents refused, insisting that their youngest son remain with them because of their great need for him. However, Allah ﷻ decreed that their mother would pass away during the month of Rajab, in the year 1360H (1942), so their father allowed him and his brother Muḥammad to study with the Shaykh two or three days a week, and then return to him.

Shaykh Ḥāfidh began to study in Sāmitah with Shaykh al-Qur'āwī, who would dictate lessons to him; after which he would return to his village. Shaykh Ḥāfidh understood and memorized everything that he read or heard. His father died while returning from Ḥajj the same year, 1360H (1942). At this time, Shaykh Ḥāfidh went and stayed with the Shaykh and began seeking knowledge fulltime.

His memory:

The older brother of Shaykh Ḥāfidh, Shaykh Muḥammad al-Ḥakami said:

Shaykh Muḥammad Abdur Razzaq Ḥamza (one of the teachers of Shaykh Ḥāfidh) visited Shaykh 'Abdullah al-Qur'āwī in Mecca during the Ḥajj season, and he brought with him two copies of the book by Imam al-Bukhārī, *The Actions of the Slaves are Created*. When Shaykh Muḥammad Ḥamza mentioned the book to Shaykh al-Qur'āwī, Shaykh Ḥāfidh let out a gasp of excitement because he yearned for this book. He had heard of this book but never seen it. After 'Ishā' prayer he requested the book from the Shaykh, so he gave him a copy. After the *Sunnah* prayers of 'Ishā' and witr; Shaykh Ḥāfidh began to copy the book in his notebook while the others slept. When the first athan for Fajr was called, his brother Muḥammad awoke to hear Shaykh Ḥāfidh saying, "May the peace and blessings of Allah be upon Muḥammad," meaning he had completed writing the entire book. The next day he returned the book to Shaykh Muḥammad Ḥamza. Shaykh Muḥammad Ḥamza said, "MashaAllah, you read the entire book?" Shaykh al-Qur'āwī responded, "No, he memorized the entire book."

His appointments and duties:

When Shaykh Ḥāfidh was only 19 years old, Shaykh al-Qur'āwī asked him to write a book about *tawhīd* and the *'aqīdah* of the Pious Predecessors that would be easy for students to memorize. Shaykh Ḥāfidh wrote a poem entitled, "*The Means of Arriving at the Knowledge of the Fundamentals of Tawhīd*," which he completed in the year 1362H (1944C.E.). This work was well received by his Shaykh and the contemporary scholars of that time. He authored other books on *tawhīd*, science of ḥadīth, Fiqh and its foundational matters, laws of inheritance and the biography of the Prophet ﷺ. His books of *'aqīdah* show a great influence from the writing of Shaykh al-Islām ibn Taymiyyah and his student Ibn al-Qayyim.

In 1363H (1945C.E.) Shaykh al-Qur'āwī selected Shaykh Ḥāfidh to be the director of the Madrassa Salafiyyah Institute in Sāmitah, which was the first and the largest of all the schools that Shaykh al-Qur'āwī established for the students of knowledge in the southern region of the kingdom. Ḥāfidh was also made regional superintendent for all the schools in the neighboring villages and townships.

Shaykh al-Qur'āwī said about him, "Indeed, he is one of my students; but he has surpassed me in knowledge."

His personality:

Shaykh Ḥāfidh had three wives, one of which was the daughter of Shaykh al-Qur'āwī.

He was thin and he loved to exercise. He was very humble and humorous with his friends and students. They all enjoyed sitting with him a great deal.

His Death:

Shaykh Ḥāfidh Al-Ḥakami remained as the director of the institute in Sāmitah until he performed Ḥajj in the year 1377H (1958C.E.). After completing the rites of Ḥajj, Shaykh Ḥāfidh died on Saturday, on the 18th of Dhul Ḥijjah, during the year 1377H (1958 C.E.), in the Mecca, from a sudden illness. He died at the young age of 35 years and three months. He was buried in Mecca ﷺ.

Translator’s Introduction

بِسْمِ اللَّهِ الرَّحْمَٰنِ الرَّحِيمِ

All praises belong to Allah, the Most Merciful, the One who sent down the Qur’an. I ask Allah, the Exalted, to elevate the rank of His final Prophet and Messenger Muḥammad ibn Abdullah ﷺ.

This tremendous book, *Advice Regarding the Book of Allah*, consists of lines of poetry by the noble scholar Shaykh Ḥāfidh al-Ḥakami ؒ. The translation of the poem is based upon the meaning explained by Shaykh Abdur Razzāq al-Badr. In the Arabic poem, each line ends with the Arabic letter “mīm.” This is understandably lost in the translation.

Rasheed ibn Estes Barbee

Rajab 1440/ March 2019

Introduction

بِسْمِ اللَّهِ الرَّحْمَٰنِ الرَّحِيمِ

All praises belong to Allāh, the One who sent His messenger ﷺ with the guidance and the true religion, to prevail over all religions. He ﷻ assisted him with clear signs, and glorious miracles. The greatest of them is the Qur'an. I bear witness that nothing has the right to be worshipped except for Allāh, alone, without any partners. All blessings and virtues come from Him. To Him belongs the best praise and all gratitude. And I bear witness that Muḥammad ﷺ is His slave and His messenger. The one He trusted with His revelation, the best of His creation, His mediator between Him and His slaves, and His argument against all mankind and *jinn*. May Allāh ﷻ exalt his rank and bestow peace upon him, his family and his companions collectively. As to what follows:

These are blessed, beneficial lines of poetry by the scholar Shaykh Ḥāfidh al-Ḥakami رحمه الله. These lines contain an explanation of the status of the Book of Allāh ﷻ, its tremendous significance and prestige, its lofty position; as well as the status of contemplating it, knowing its rulings, working according to its rulings, and believing in the verses that are not entirely clear. Likewise, in these lines of poetry, he mentioned the virtues of reciting the Qur'an often, in addition to a number of great benefits connected to the Book of Allāh ﷻ.

This is a section I singled out from what is contained in the *mīmiya* poem of advice concerning manners and knowledge. I have a printed explanation of this poem. However, some of the noble brothers desired this portion of the book to be separated, along with its explanation, to make it easy to circulate and distribute; especially in the circles of Qur'an memorization. We hope Allāh ﷻ will maximize the blessing and benefit. Verily, He hears all and responds to the supplications.

Written by Abdur Razzāq al-Badr

Reciting the Qur'an with Contemplation and a Slow, Measured Recital

Poem

وَبِالتَّدَبُّرِ والتَّرتيلِ فَاتْلُ كِتا بَ اللهِ لاسِيَّما في حِنْدسِ الظُّلَمِ

And with contemplation and a slow, measured recital, thus recite the Book of Allāh, especially during the pitch-black darkness.

Explanation

In his statement, "With contemplation and a slow, measured recital," the preposition and the noun following it are connected to his statement, thus recite the Book of Allāh," meaning recite the Book of Allāh with contemplation and a slow, measured recital. Allāh has commanded us to reflect and contemplate His Book in various verses in the Qur'an. Allāh the Exalted said:

﴿ أَفَلَا يَتَدَبَّرُونَ الْقُرْآنَ ۚ وَلَوْ كَانَ مِنْ عِندِ غَيْرِ اللَّهِ لَوَجَدُوا فِيهِ اخْتِلَافًا كَثِيرًا ﴿٨٢﴾ ﴾

Do they not then contemplate the Qur'an carefully? Had it been from other than Allāh, they would surely have found therein many contradictions.[1]

And the Exalted said:

﴿ أَفَلَا يَتَدَبَّرُونَ الْقُرْآنَ أَمْ عَلَىٰ قُلُوبٍ أَقْفَالُهَا ﴿٢٤﴾ ﴾

Then do they not reflect upon the Qur'an, or are there locks upon [their] hearts?[2]

And the Exalted said:

﴿ أَفَلَمْ يَدَّبَّرُوا الْقَوْلَ أَمْ جَاءَهُم مَّا لَمْ يَأْتِ آبَاءَهُمُ الْأَوَّلِينَ ﴿٦٨﴾ ﴾

Have they not pondered over the Word or has there come to them what had not come to their fathers of old?[3]

And the Exalted said:

﴿ كِتَابٌ أَنزَلْنَاهُ إِلَيْكَ مُبَارَكٌ لِّيَدَّبَّرُوا آيَاتِهِ وَلِيَتَذَكَّرَ أُولُو الْأَلْبَابِ ﴿٢٩﴾ ﴾

(This is) a Book (the Qur'an) which We have sent down to you, full of blessings, that they may ponder

[1] Sūrah an-Nisā', 4:82
[2] Sūrah Muḥammad, 47:24
[3] Sūrah al-Mu'minūn, 23:68

over its Verses, and that men of understanding may remember.[1]

These verses incite us to contemplate the Book of Allāh ﷻ. Contemplating is implemented by reflecting over its meanings, pondering its guidance, and comprehending the intent of Allāh, the Exalted, such that the slave's portion from the Qur'an includes his recitation of the letters, and understanding its meanings and guidance. And his portion is not merely reciting the letters properly.

His statement, "a slow, measured recital," means a recitation that is deliberate; because this will assist you in understand and pondering it. There is a difference between the individual who recites a chapter of the Qur'an while he wants to comprehend what Allāh ﷻ is saying to him in these verses, and the individual who recites it while he wants to finish it and relieve himself of its recitation.

The poet رحمه الله began with an incitement to recite the Qur'an with contemplation and a slow, measured recital. This advice is in accordance with many verses in the Book of Allāh ﷻ, and a number of *aḥadīth* found in the sunnah of the Prophet ﷺ. The Qur'an comes with an incitement to give great concern to reciting the Qur'an with and slow, measured recital, and reflection and contemplation. Allāh, the Exalted, said:

﴿وَاتْلُ مَا أُوحِيَ إِلَيْكَ مِن كِتَابِ رَبِّكَ ﴿٢٧﴾﴾

And recite what has been revealed to you of the Book of your Lord.[2]

[1] Sūrah Ṣād, 38:29
[2] Sūrah al-Kahf, 18:27

And He said:

﴿ الَّذِينَ آتَيْنَاهُمُ الْكِتَابَ يَتْلُونَهُ حَقَّ تِلَاوَتِهِ أُولَٰئِكَ يُؤْمِنُونَ بِهِ ﴿١٢١﴾ ﴾

Those to whom We have given the Book recite it with its true recital. They [are the ones who] believe in it.[1]

And His statement:

﴿ لَيْسُوا سَوَاءً ۗ مِّنْ أَهْلِ الْكِتَابِ أُمَّةٌ قَائِمَةٌ يَتْلُونَ آيَاتِ اللَّهِ آنَاءَ اللَّيْلِ وَهُمْ يَسْجُدُونَ ﴿١١٣﴾ ﴾

Not all of them are alike; a party of the people of the Scripture stand for the right, they recite the Verses of Allāh during the hours of the night, prostrating themselves in prayer.[2]

And His statement:

﴿ إِنَّ الَّذِينَ يَتْلُونَ كِتَابَ اللَّهِ وَأَقَامُوا الصَّلَاةَ وَأَنفَقُوا مِمَّا رَزَقْنَاهُمْ سِرًّا وَعَلَانِيَةً يَرْجُونَ تِجَارَةً لَّن تَبُورَ ﴿٢٩﴾ ﴾

Verily, those who recite the Book of Allāh, and establish the prayer, and spend (in charity) out of what

---

[1] Sūrah al-Baqarah, 2:121

[2] Sūrah 'Āli 'Imrān, 3:113

We have provided for them, secretly and openly, hope for a (sure) trade gain that will never perish.[1]

The verses with this meaning are numerous. Likewise, there are *aḥadīth* in the Sunnah that incite recitation of the Qur'an with a recitation that is slow and deliberate, with reflection; along with mentioning the virtue of doing so. The Prophet peace be upon him said:

مَثَلُ الَّذِي يَقْرَأُ الْقُرْآنَ كَالأُتْرُجَّةِ طَعْمُهَا طَيِّبٌ وَرِيحُهَا طَيِّبٌ

The example of the person who recites the Qur'an is like that of a citron which tastes good and smells good.[2]

The Prophet ﷺ said to his companions:

أَيُّكُمْ يُحِبُّ أَنْ يَغْدُوَ كُلَّ يَوْمٍ إِلَى بُطْحَانَ أَوْ إِلَى الْعَقِيقِ فَيَأْتِيَ مِنْهُ بِنَاقَتَيْنِ كَوْمَاوَيْنِ فِي غَيْرِ إِثْمٍ وَلاَ قَطْعِ رَحِمٍ". فَقُلْنَا يَا رَسُولَ اللَّهِ نُحِبُّ ذَلِكَ . قَالَ " أَفَلاَ يَغْدُو أَحَدُكُمْ إِلَى الْمَسْجِدِ فَيَعْلَمَ أَوْ يَقْرَأَ آيَتَيْنِ مِنْ كِتَابِ اللَّهِ عَزَّ وَجَلَّ خَيْرٌ لَهُ مِنْ نَاقَتَيْنِ وَثَلاَثٌ خَيْرٌ لَهُ مِنْ ثَلاَثٍ وَأَرْبَعٌ خَيْرٌ لَهُ مِنْ أَرْبَعٍ وَمِنْ أَعْدَادِهِنَّ مِنَ الإِبِلِ

Which of you would love to go out every morning to Buthan or Al-'Aqiq and bring two large-humped, fat she-camels without being guilty of sin or severing ties of relationship? They said, "Messenger of Allāh, we would all love that." He said, "If any one of you goes out in the morning to the *masjid* and learns or recites two verses from the Book of Allāh ﷻ, it is better for him than two she-camels. And three verses are better for him than three she-camels,

---

[1] Sūrah Fāṭir, 35:29

[2] Ṣaḥīḥ al-Bukhārī, 5020

and four verses are better for him than four camels, and so on to the corresponding numbers in camels."[1]

And he ﷺ said:

مَا اجْتَمَعَ قَوْمٌ فِي بَيْتٍ مِنْ بُيُوتِ اللَّهِ تَعَالَى يَتْلُونَ كِتَابَ اللَّهِ وَيَتَدَارَسُونَهُ بَيْنَهُمْ إِلاَّ نَزَلَتْ عَلَيْهِمُ السَّكِينَةُ وَغَشِيَتْهُمُ الرَّحْمَةُ وَحَفَّتْهُمُ الْمَلاَئِكَةُ وَذَكَرَهُمُ اللَّهُ فِيمَنْ عِنْدَهُ

No people gather together in a house of the houses of Allāh, the most high , reciting the Book of Allāh, and learning it together among themselves, except that calmness descends upon them, mercy covers them, the angels surround them, and Allāh makes a mention of them among those who are with Him.[2]

And his ﷺ statement:

مَنْ قَرَأَ حَرْفًا مِنْ كِتَابِ اللَّهِ فَلَهُ بِهِ حَسَنَةٌ وَالْحَسَنَةُ بِعَشْرِ أَمْثَالِهَا لاَ أَقُولُ الم حَرْفٌ وَلَكِنْ أَلِفٌ حَرْفٌ وَلاَمٌ حَرْفٌ وَمِيمٌ حَرْفٌ

Whoever recites a letter from the Book of Allāh will have a good deed, and a good deed of ten the like of it. I do not say that alif lām mīm is a letter, but alif is a letter, lām is a letter and mīm is a letter.[3]

The poet رحمه الله said, "especially during the pitch-black darkness," meaning especially during this blessed time.

---

[1] Ṣaḥīḥ Muslim, 803
[2] Sunan Abi Dāwūd, 1455
[3] Tirmidhī, 2910

Imam Nawawī ﷺ said in *Clarifying the Manners of Carrying the Qur'an*, in the chapter "The Preferred Time to Recite", "Know that the best time for recitation is recitation within the prayer. As for recitation outside of the prayer, then the best recitation is during the night; and the last part of the night is better than the first part of the night.[1]

[1] Page 75

Working and Ruling by the Qur'an

Poem

حَكِّمْ بَرَاهِينَهُ واعْمَلْ بِمُحْكَمِهِ حِلًّا وحَظْرًا وما قَدْ حَدَّهُ أَقِمِ

Judge according to its proofs; and work according its clear evidences in those matters which are permissible and impermissible, and establish its limits.

Explanation

"Judge according to its proofs"; its proofs means its arguments and manifest signs. This means you must judge according to the Qur'an, such that you rely upon it in all your affairs.

"Work according to its clear evidences"; the word *muḥkam* means its clear proofs and evidences. Allāh, the Exalted, said:

﴿ هُوَ الَّذِي أَنزَلَ عَلَيْكَ الْكِتَابَ مِنْهُ آيَاتٌ مُّحْكَمَاتٌ هُنَّ أُمُّ الْكِتَابِ وَأُخَرُ مُتَشَابِهَاتٌ ﴿٧﴾ ﴾

It is He Who has sent down to you (Muḥammad) the Book. In it are Verses that are entirely clear, they are

the foundations of the Book; and others not entirely clear.[1]

"In those matters which are permissible and impermissible"; the word *ḥaẓr* means something prohibited. Thus, be from those who work according to the Qur'an, as it relates to the permissible and impermissible matters; those matters that are allowed and those that are prohibited.

"And establish its limits," meaning uphold the limits and boundaries of the Qur'an, and do not let your upholding the limits of the Qur'an be restricted to its letters. Rather, establish the proper recitation of its letters; and also uphold its boundaries and limits by working according to what is found in the Qur'an, and avoiding what it prohibits.

Abdur Razzāq[2] narrated in his book of *ḥadīth,* the *tafsīr* from Ḥasan al-Baṣrī, concerning the statement of Allāh, the Exalted:

﴿ كِتَابٌ أَنزَلْنَاهُ إِلَيْكَ مُبَارَكٌ لِّيَدَّبَّرُوا آيَاتِهِ وَلِيَتَذَكَّرَ أُولُو الْأَلْبَابِ ﴿٢٩﴾ ﴾

(This is) a Book (the Qur'an) which We have sent down to you, full of blessings, that they may ponder over its Verses, and that men of understanding may remember.[3]

"There is no pondering over the verses of the Qur'an except by following it and by working according to it. I swear by Allāh ﷻ, it is not by memorizing its letters while neglecting its limits. A person will say, 'By Allāh,

---

[1] Sūrah 'Āli 'Imrān, 3:7

[2] Translator's note: He is the noble scholar Abdur Razzāq ibn Hammam ibn Nafi' al-Ṣan'ānī, born 126 years after the migration.

[3] Sūrah Ṣād, 38:29

I have recited the entire Qur'an and I have not neglected a single letter,' while in reality he has neglected the entire Qur'an. The Qur'an cannot be seen in his manners or his actions. One of them will say, 'By Allāh, I will recite a sūrah from the Qur'an in a single breath, I swear by Allāh!' These individuals are not reciters, scholars, people of wisdom, or people of piety. Since when did reciters say the likes of this speech?! May Allāh ﷻ not increase Muslims like this."

A Warning Against Speaking About the Qur'an with Mere Opinion

Poem

واطْلُبْ مَعانِيهِ بالنَّقْلِ الصّريحِ ولا تَخُضْ بِرَأيِكَ واحْذَرْ بَطْشَ مُنْتَقِمِ

Seek its meanings by way of clear text, and do not embark upon it with your opinion, and beware of the might of the One who takes revenge.

Explanation

Search for the meanings of the Qur'an and its evidences with clear texts. Parts of the Qur'an explain other parts, and the *Sunnah* is the explainer and interpreter for the Qur'an. This is the methodology of the scholars in explaining the Qur'an. They interpret the Qur'an using the Qur'an. They interpret the Qur'an using authentic *aḥadīth* from the Messenger of Allāh ﷺ. And they interpret the Qur'an using narrations from the companions; the people who witnessed the revelation. Allāh ﷻ honored the companions by allowing them to receive the Qur'an directly from the Messenger of Allāh ﷺ.

"Do not embark upon it with your opinion," meaning do not work based upon your mere opinion when it comes to the Book of Allāh ﷻ. And do not speak about the Qur'an with your opinion. Your view must be based upon the clear text. The Shaykh ﷀ gave a severe warning against using opinion as it relates to the Qur'an.

He said, "Beware of the might of the One who takes revenge," meaning beware of the might of Allāh ﷻ and His punishment; and do not speak about His Book without knowledge. Allāh, the Exalted, said:

﴿ قُلْ إِنَّمَا حَرَّمَ رَبِّيَ الْفَوَاحِشَ مَا ظَهَرَ مِنْهَا وَمَا بَطَنَ وَالْإِثْمَ وَالْبَغْيَ بِغَيْرِ الْحَقِّ وَأَن تُشْرِكُوا بِاللَّهِ مَا لَمْ يُنَزِّلْ بِهِ سُلْطَانًا وَأَن تَقُولُوا عَلَى اللَّهِ مَا لَا تَعْلَمُونَ ﴿٣٣﴾ ﴾

Say, "My Lord has only forbidden immoralities—what is apparent of them and what is concealed—and sin, and oppression without right, and that you associate with Allāh that for which He has not sent down authority, and that you say about Allāh that which you do not know.[1]"

And the Exalted said:

﴿ وَلَا تَقْفُ مَا لَيْسَ لَكَ بِهِ عِلْمٌ ۚ إِنَّ السَّمْعَ وَالْبَصَرَ وَالْفُؤَادَ كُلُّ أُولَٰئِكَ كَانَ عَنْهُ مَسْئُولًا ﴿٣٦﴾ ﴾

[1] Sūrah al-'A'rāf, 7:33

And follow not that of which you have no knowledge. Verily, the hearing, and the sight, and the heart, of each of those you will be questioned (by Allāh).[1]

Allāh, the Exalted, said:

﴿أَلَمْ يُؤْخَذْ عَلَيْهِم مِّيثَاقُ الْكِتَابِ أَن لَّا يَقُولُوا عَلَى اللَّهِ إِلَّا الْحَقَّ ﴿١٦٩﴾﴾

Was not the covenant of the Book taken from them, that they would not say about Allāh anything but the truth?[2]

For this reason, the companions, and those who followed them in goodness, had the utmost and complete piety and fear against explaining the Qur'an with mere opinion and conjecture. Ibn Abī Shaibah[3] narrated in his book of *ḥadīth*, from Abu Bakr aṣ-Ṣiddiq ﷺ, that he was asked about the statement of Allāh, the Exalted:

﴿وَفَاكِهَةً وَأَبًّا ﴿٣١﴾﴾

And fruit and grass.[4]

---

[1] Sūrah al-'Isrā', 18:36

[2] Sūrah al-'A'rāf, 7:169

[3] Translator's note: He is the noble scholar of *ḥadīth*, born 159 years after the migration.

[4] Sūrah 'Abasa, 80:31

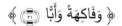

He said, "What heaven will shelter me, and what earth will conceal me, if I speak about the Book of Allāh ﷻ concerning that which I have no knowledge?"

The narrations similar to this are numerous.

Return the Unclear Verses to the Clear Verses

Poem

فمَا عَلِمْتَ بِمَحْضِ النَّقْلِ مِنْهُ فَقُلْ وَكِلْ إِلَى اللهِ مَعْنى كلِّ مُنْبَهِمِ

That which you know is from the pure text, then say; and entrust to Allāh the meaning of everything which is ambiguous.

Explanation

That which is clear to you, and the intent of it is clear, then say, "This means such and such," while relying and utilizing the particular text that clarified the meaning and the intent to you. His intent by "the text" is that you rely on the text in this matter, and this is the methodology of the scholars in dealing with the unclear verses in the Qur'an. They return the unclear verses to the clear verses. And Allāh ﷻ has commanded us to do this. He, the Exalted, said:

﴿ هُوَ الَّذِي أَنزَلَ عَلَيْكَ الْكِتَابَ مِنْهُ آيَاتٌ مُّحْكَمَاتٌ هُنَّ أُمُّ الْكِتَابِ

وَأُخَرُ مُتَشَابِهَاتٌ ﴿٧﴾ ﴾

It is He Who has sent down to you (Muḥammad) the Book. In it are Verses that are entirely clear, they are the foundations of the Book; and others not entirely clear.[1]

He described the clear verses as the "Mother of the Book".

"Entrust to Allāh ﷻ the meaning of everything which is ambiguous," meaning the verses with meaning that are unclear or hidden to you. Then entrust its meaning to Allāh by saying, "Allāh knows best what it means."

Masruq ؓ said:

كُنَّا عِنْدَ عَبْدِ اللَّهِ جُلُوسًا وَهُوَ مُضْطَجِعٌ بَيْنَنَا فَأَتَاهُ رَجُلٌ فَقَالَ يَا أَبَا عَبْدِ الرَّحْمَنِ إِنَّ قَاصًّا عِنْدَ أَبْوَابِ كِنْدَةَ يَقُصُّ وَيَزْعُمُ أَنَّ آيَةَ الدُّخَانِ تَجِيءُ فَتَأْخُذُ بِأَنْفَاسِ الْكُفَّارِ وَيَأْخُذُ الْمُؤْمِنِينَ مِنْهُ كَهَيْئَةِ الزُّكَامِ فَقَالَ عَبْدُ اللَّهِ وَجَلَسَ وَهُوَ غَضْبَانُ يَا أَيُّهَا النَّاسُ اتَّقُوا اللَّهَ مَنْ عَلِمَ مِنْكُمْ شَيْئًا فَلْيَقُلْ بِمَا يَعْلَمُ وَمَنْ لَمْ يَعْلَمْ فَلْيَقُلِ اللَّهُ أَعْلَمُ فَإِنَّهُ أَعْلَمُ لأَحَدِكُمْ أَنْ يَقُولَ لِمَا لاَ يَعْلَمُ اللَّهُ أَعْلَمُ فَإِنَّ اللَّهَ عَزَّ وَجَلَّ قَالَ لِنَبِيِّهِ صلى الله عليه وسلم ﴿قُلْ مَا أَسْأَلُكُمْ عَلَيْهِ مِنْ أَجْرٍ وَمَا أَنَا مِنَ الْمُتَكَلِّفِينَ ﴿٨٦﴾﴾

We were sitting in the company of Abdullah[2], and he was lying down when someone came and said, "O Abdur Rahman, a story-teller at the gates of Kinda[3] is narrating his belief that the verse which deals with the smoke implies that the smoke would take the

---

[1] Sūrah 'Āli `Imrān, 3:7

[2] Translator's note: Meaning the noble companion Abdullah ibn Masood may Allah be pleased with him.

[3] Translator's note: A gate in Kūfah

breath of the disbelievers and would inflict the believers with cold." Abdullah sat up and said in anger, "O people, fear Allāh. Whoever knows something should say only what he knows, and whoever does not know should say, 'Allāh knows best.' It is most knowledgeable for one of you, if he does not know something to say, 'Allāh knows best'. Allāh ﷻ said to His Prophet ﷺ, 'Say[1] (O Muḥammad), "No wage do I ask of you for this (the Qur'an), nor am I one of those who pretends and fabricates things which do not exist." '[2]

Ibn Umar ؓ said, "Knowledge is found in three: the Qur'an, the *Sunnah* and saying, 'I do not know.'"[3]

---

[1] Sūrah Ṣād, 38:86
[2] Ṣaḥīḥ Muslim, 2798
[3] Collected by Ṭabarānī, 251

A Warning Against Argumentation Concerning the Qur'an

Poem

ثُمَّ الْمِرَا فيه كُفْرٌ فاحْذَرَنْهُ ولا يَسْتَهْوِيَنَّكَ أقوامٌ بِزَيْغِهِمِ

Disputing concerning it is disbelief; thus, beware of it, and do not allow people to seduce you with their deviance.

Explanation

"Disputing concerning it," meaning concerning the Qur'an. Disputing means debate and argumentation which leads to doubt, rejection of the Qur'an and baseless beliefs in creed.

"Disbelief," this alludes to what has been collected by Imam Aḥmad from the *ḥadīth* of Abu Huraira. The Messenger of Allāh ﷺ said:

نزل القرآنُ على سبعةِ أحرفٍ المراءُ في القرآنِ كفرٌ ثلاثَ مراتٍ فما عُلِّمْتُمْ فاعملُوا به وما جَهِلْتُمْ منه فردُّوهُ إلى عالِمِهِ

The Qur'an was sent down with seven dialects. Disputing concerning the Qur'an is disbelief (he repeated this three times). Therefore, that which you know from the Qur'an, then implement; and that which you are ignorant of, then return it to the One who has knowledge of it.[1]

The statement of the Prophet ﷺ, "That which you are ignorant of, then return it to the One who has knowledge of it," is the point of reference of the poet that we covered in the previous section; "and entrust to Allāh the meaning of everything which is ambiguous."

Abu Dāwūd aṭ-Ṭayālisī[2] collected a *ḥadīth* from ibn 'Umar, that the Prophet ibn Umar said:

لا تُجادِلوا في القرآنِ ، فإنَّ جدالًا فيه كُفْرٌ

Do not dispute concerning the Qur'an, because disputing concerning it is disbelief.[3]

"Thus, beware of it," meaning be cautious of that, and beware of falling into anything of dispute concerning the Book of Allāh the Exalted; because this leads to rejection of it, doubt and disbelief in Allāh ﷻ and His Book!

"Do not allow people to seduce you with their deviance," often the people of deviance put the people to trial by beautifying the deviance and

---

[1] Aḥmad, 7989; declared authentic by Shaykh al-Albānī

[2] Translator's note: He is the noble scholar Abu Dāwūd Sulaymān ibn Dāwūd aṭ-Ṭayālisī, born 133 years after migration.

[3] Collected in the Musnad of aṭ-Ṭayālisī, 2286; declared authentic by Shaykh al-Albānī.

misguidance they are upon using beautified speech. Thus, those with weak faith and little knowledge will be put to trial. So he warned against the person being placed into *fitnah* by the likes of these people.

Implement the Commands of the Qur'an and Avoid Its Prohibitions

POEM

وعنْ مَناهِيهِ كُنْ يا صاحِ مُنْزَجِرًا والأمْرُ منهُ بلا تِردادٍ فالْتَزِم

From its prohibitions, "Be, O my comrade, one who refrains; and, with its commands, without hesitation, adhere to them."

EXPLANATION

"From its prohibitions, "Be, O my comrade, one who refrains," meaning be of those who refrain and abstain from everything Allāh ﷻ has prohibited in the Qur'an.

"And, with its commands, without hesitation, adhere to them," meaning implement, guard, and adhere to the commands. Commands are something that is put into practice; therefore, obey them.

In these lines of poetry, he combines the incitement to implement the commands, while avoiding the prohibitions. Ibn Masūd ؓ said, "When you hear Allāh saying, 'O you who believe,' give it your full attention because it is either some good you are being commanded with, or some evil you are being prohibited from."[1]

This reminds me of a young boy I taught almost twenty years ago. At this time, he was in middle school and he had memorized the Book of Allāh ﷻ. He came to me one day with some papers and written on them were the commands and prohibitions from the Qur'an. He said to me, "This is something I compiled, and I want you to look over it." I replied to him, "You are still young, and you are already authoring works?" He said, "No, I did not author it; but Allāh ﷻ favored me to memorize the Qur'an, and when I read the Qur'an I pass by many commands and prohibitions which Allāh addresses me with. So I wanted to comprehend what Allāh ﷻ is commanding me with, and what He is prohibiting me from." Every time he came across a command or a prohibition, he would write it down and then review the *tafsīr* of ibn Kathīr or the *tafsīr* of as-Sa'dī. He did this until he had compiled a huge section about the knowledge of commands and prohibitions.

---

[1] Collected by ibn Abī Ḥātim in his *tafsīr* of this verse (1/196)

Unclear Verses in the Qur'an

Poem

وما تَشابَهَ فَوِّضْ لِلإلَهَ وَلا تَخُضْ فَخَوْضُكَ فيه مُوجِبُ النِّقَمِ

That which is unclear, then entrust it to its God; and do not delve into it, because your delving into it will cause punishment.

Explanation

Here he explains the correct methodology concerning the unclear verses in the Qur'an.

Allāh, the Exalted, said:

﴿ هُوَ الَّذِي أَنزَلَ عَلَيْكَ الْكِتَابَ مِنْهُ آيَاتٌ مُّحْكَمَاتٌ هُنَّ أُمُّ الْكِتَابِ
وَأُخَرُ مُتَشَابِهَاتٌ ﴿٧﴾ ﴾

It is He Who has sent down to you (Muḥammad) the Book. In it are Verses that are entirely clear, they are

the foundations of the Book; and others not entirely clear.[1]

The Qur'an has verses which are not entirely clear; the unclear verses are the opposite of the clear verses. The clear verses have meanings which are completely clear, with obvious evidence. The unclear verses are those where the meaning is not completely clear.

The "unclear verses" means these verses are unclear to some people; it does not mean these verses are unrestrictedly unclear. This is because there is no verse in the Qur'an in which the meaning is unrestrictedly ambiguous. Allāh ﷻ addresses us using the clear Arabic language, so there does not exist a verse in which the meaning is hidden to each and every individual.

Mujāhid[2] ﷺ said, "I went through the *muṣḥaf* (the Qur'an) with Ibn 'Abbas three times, from Sūrah al-Fātiḥah to the end. I stopped at each verse and asked him about it.[3]

Ibn 'Abbas ﷺ said, "Explanation of the Qur'an is of four types. The explanation that no one is excused for not knowing it, the explanation known by the Arab-speaking people by way of the language, the explanation known by the scholars who are firmly grounded in knowledge,

---

[1] Sūrah 'Āli 'Imrān, 3:7

[2] Translator's note: He is Mujāhid ibn Jabr, the noble scholar of *tafsīr*; from the second generation, born 22 years after the migration.

[3] Collected by Ibn Jarīr aṭ-Ṭabarī in his *tafsīr*, 4337

and the explanation only known by Allāh. Ibn Kathīr said this statement has been narrated from ʻĀ'isha, ʻUrwa[1], Abu ash-Sha'thā'[2], Abu Nahīk[3].

The statement of Ibn ʻAbbas, "the explanation known by the scholars who are firmly grounded in knowledge," this is the meaning of the unclear verses, as Allāh, the Exalted, said:

﴿ هُوَ الَّذِي أَنزَلَ عَلَيْكَ الْكِتَابَ مِنْهُ آيَاتٌ مُّحْكَمَاتٌ هُنَّ أُمُّ الْكِتَابِ وَأُخَرُ مُتَشَابِهَاتٌ ۖ فَأَمَّا الَّذِينَ فِي قُلُوبِهِمْ زَيْغٌ فَيَتَّبِعُونَ مَا تَشَابَهَ مِنْهُ ابْتِغَاءَ الْفِتْنَةِ وَابْتِغَاءَ تَأْوِيلِهِ ۗ وَمَا يَعْلَمُ تَأْوِيلَهُ إِلَّا اللَّهُ ۗ وَالرَّاسِخُونَ فِي الْعِلْمِ ﴿٧﴾ ﴾

It is He Who has sent down to you (Muḥammad) the Book. In it are Verses that are entirely clear, they are the foundations of the Book; and others not entirely clear. So as for those in whose hearts there is a deviation, they follow that which is not entirely clear thereof, seeking trials and tribulations, and seeking for its hidden meanings; but none knows its hidden meanings except Allāh, and those who are firmly grounded in knowledge.[4]

[1] Translator's note: He is the noble scholar ʻUrwa, the son of Zubayr ibn al-ʻAwwam and Asmā' bint Abu Bakr. He was born 23 years after the migration.

[2] Translator's note: He is the noble scholar from the second generation, Jābir ibn Zayd, born 21 years after the migration.

[3] Translator's note: Abu Nahīk is from the noble companions.

[4] Sūrah 'Āli ʻImrān, 3:7

Those who are firmly grounded in knowledge know the meaning of the unclear verses. They know the meanings that are hidden from many of the people, due to what Allāh ﷻ has given them of insight and understanding of the Speech of Allāh, the Exalted; and due to their returning the unclear verses back to the clear verses.

As for the *tafsīr* that is only known to Allāh ﷻ, it is the true reality of His Attributes, the true reality of the Day of Judgement and other affairs mentioned in the Book of Allāh and the Sunnah of His Prophet ﷺ. The meanings and evidences of these matters are known; while the true nature, essence and reality are hidden.

As Ibn 'Abbas ﷺ said, "There is nothing in this world similar to anything in Paradise except for the names."[1]

Thus, we know the meaning and the evidences, but the true nature and reality is only known to Allāh ﷻ.

---

[1] Collected by ibn Jarir in his *tafsīr*, 535

A Warning from the People of Deviance, Innovation and Misguidance

Poem

ولا تُطِعْ قولَ ذي زيْغٍ يُزَخْرِفُهُ مِنْ كُلِّ مُبْتَدِعٍ في الدين مُتَّهَمِ

حَيْرانَ ضلَّ عنِ الحقِّ الْمُبينِ فلا يَنْفَكُّ مُنْحَرِفًا مُعْوَجَّ لَمْ يَقُمِ

Do not obey the statement of the deviant who adorns it; from each and every innovator in the religion who is guilty, confused, and misguided from the clear truth. Thus, he will not disengage from his deviant crookedness and he will not be upright.

Explanation

In these two lines of poetry, the Shaykh ﷺ warns against the path of the people of desires, the people who are destroyed, and the people of deviance and misguidance. He warns against listening to them.

He said, "Do not obey the statement of the deviant who adorns it." It is from the behavior of the people of deviance to adorn the falsehood they are upon. Allāh, the Exalted, said:

﴿ وَلَا تُطِعْ مَنْ أَغْفَلْنَا قَلْبَهُ عَن ذِكْرِنَا وَاتَّبَعَ هَوَاهُ وَكَانَ أَمْرُهُ فُرُطًا ﴿٢٨﴾ ﴾

And obey not him whose heart We have made heedless of Our Remembrance, one who follows his own lusts and whose affair (deeds) has been lost.[1]

'Ā'isha ﷺ said, The Messenger of Allāh ﷺ recited the verse:

﴿ هُوَ الَّذِي أَنزَلَ عَلَيْكَ الْكِتَابَ مِنْهُ آيَاتٌ مُّحْكَمَاتٌ هُنَّ أُمُّ الْكِتَابِ وَأُخَرُ مُتَشَابِهَاتٌ ۖ فَأَمَّا الَّذِينَ فِي قُلُوبِهِمْ زَيْغٌ فَيَتَّبِعُونَ مَا تَشَابَهَ مِنْهُ ابْتِغَاءَ الْفِتْنَةِ وَابْتِغَاءَ تَأْوِيلِهِ ۗ وَمَا يَعْلَمُ تَأْوِيلَهُ إِلَّا اللَّهُ ۗ وَالرَّاسِخُونَ فِي الْعِلْمِ يَقُولُونَ آمَنَّا بِهِ كُلٌّ مِّنْ عِندِ رَبِّنَا ۗ وَمَا يَذَّكَّرُ إِلَّا أُولُو الْأَلْبَابِ ﴿٧﴾ ﴾

It is He Who has sent down to you (Muḥammad) the Book. In it are Verses that are entirely clear; they are the foundations of the Book, and others not entirely clear. So as for those in whose hearts there is a deviation, they follow that which is not entirely clear thereof, seeking trials and tribulations, and seeking for its hidden meanings. But none knows its hidden meanings except Allāh; and those who are firmly grounded in knowledge say, "We believe in

---

[1] Sūrah al-Kahf, 18:28

it, the whole of it (clear and unclear verses) are from our Lord." And none receive admonition except men of understanding.[1]

Then the Messenger of Allāh ﷺ said:

فَإِذَا رَأَيْتُمُ الَّذِينَ يَتَّبِعُونَ مَا تَشَابَهَ مِنْهُ فَأُولَئِكَ الَّذِينَ سَمَّى اللَّهُ فَاحْذَرُوهُمْ

When you see those people following the unclear verses, they are those whom Allāh has named, so beware of them.[2]

"From each and every innovator in the religion who is guilty," meaning be cautious of the people of deviance; to include the innovator, and people of desires who are guilty of corruption in the Islamic creed or weak in their concepts.

"Confused, misguided from the clear truth," he describes the condition of the deviant innovators. And how often does this confusion seize the people of falsehood!

"Thus, he will not disengage from his deviant crookedness," meaning he will be in this condition always; forever astray from the straight path of Allāh ﷻ, crooked away from the upright road.

"He will not be upright," meaning he will not be upright upon the path of Allāh ﷻ, rather he will stray to the right and the left.

---

[1] Sūrah 'Āli 'Imrān, 3:7

[2] Sunan Abi Dāwūd, 4598

It Is as Though the Reciter of the Qur'an is Addressing the Most Merciful

Poem

هُوَ الكِتابُ الذي مَن قامَ يَقْرَؤُهُ كَأنَّما خاطَبَ الرَّحْمَنَ بالكَلِمِ

It is the Book which the one who stands reciting it, it is as though he is addressing the Most Merciful with words.

Explanation

It is as though the person who reads the Speech of Allāh ﷻ is addressing the Most Merciful with words, because the Qur'an—all of it—is glorification of Allāh, supplication to Him, and praising and magnifying Him. This is found in the mother of the Qur'an, the opening chapter of the Book, as it contains in general what the remainder of the Qur'an contains in detail. It contains supplicating and praising Allāh ﷻ.

Abu Huraira ﵁ said, I heard the Messenger of Allāh ﷺ saying:

قَالَ اللَّهُ عَزَّ وَجَلَّ قَسَمْتُ الصَّلاَةَ بَيْنِي وَبَيْنَ عَبْدِي شَطْرَيْنِ فَنِصْفُهَا لِي وَنِصْفُهَا لِعَبْدِي وَلِعَبْدِي مَا سَأَلَ " . قَالَ فَقَالَ رَسُولُ اللَّهِ . صلى الله عليه وسلم . " اقْرَءُوا يَقُولُ الْعَبْدُ {الْحَمْدُ لِلَّهِ رَبِّ الْعَالَمِينَ} فَيَقُولُ اللَّهُ عَزَّ وَجَلَّ حَمِدَنِي عَبْدِي وَلِعَبْدِي مَا سَأَلَ . فَيَقُولُ {الرَّحْمَنِ الرَّحِيمِ} فَيَقُولُ أَثْنَى عَلَىَّ عَبْدِي وَلِعَبْدِي مَا سَأَلَ . يَقُولُ {مَالِكِ يَوْمِ الدِّينِ } فَيَقُولُ اللَّهُ مَجَّدَنِي عَبْدِي فَهَذَا لِي وَهَذِهِ الآيَةُ بَيْنِي وَبَيْنَ عَبْدِي نِصْفَيْنِ يَقُولُ الْعَبْدُ {إِيَّاكَ نَعْبُدُ وَإِيَّاكَ نَسْتَعِينُ} يَعْنِي فَهَذِهِ بَيْنِي وَبَيْنَ عَبْدِي وَلِعَبْدِي مَا سَأَلَ وَآخِرُ السُّورَةِ لِعَبْدِي يَقُولُ الْعَبْدُ {اهْدِنَا الصِّرَاطَ الْمُسْتَقِيمَ * صِرَاطَ الَّذِينَ أَنْعَمْتَ عَلَيْهِمْ غَيْرِ الْمَغْضُوبِ عَلَيْهِمْ وَلاَ الضَّالِّينَ} فَهَذَا لِعَبْدِي وَلِعَبْدِي مَا سَأَلَ

Allāh ﷺ said: I have divided prayer between Myself and My slave into two halves, and My slave shall have what he has asked for. When the slave says: "All the praises and thanks be to Allāh, the Lord of all that exists," Allāh says: "My slave has praised Me." And when he says: "The Most Beneficent, the Most Merciful", Allāh says: "My slave has extolled Me." And when he says: "The Only Owner of the Day of Recompense," Allāh says: "My slave has glorified Me." And on one occasion He said: "My slave has submitted to My power." And when he says: "You (Alone) we worship, and You (Alone) we ask for help," He says: "This is between Me and My slave, and My slave shall have what he is asking for." And when he says: "Guide us to the Straight Way. The way of those on whom You have bestowed Your Grace, not (the way) of those who earned

Your Anger, nor of those who went astray," He says: "This is for My slave, and My slave shall have what he has asked for."[1]

---

[1] Muslim, 395

Descriptions of the Noble Qur'an

Poem

هُوَ الصِّراطُ هُو الْحَبْلُ الْمَتِينُ هُوَ الْ ميزانُ والعُرْوَةُ الوُثْقَى لِمُعْتَصِمِ

It is the path, it is the strong rope, it is the scale; it is the trustworthy handhold for those who adhere to it.

Explanation

"It is the path," meaning it is the straight path that will lead its companion to the garden of bliss.

﴿ وَأَنَّ هَٰذَا صِرَاطِي مُسْتَقِيمًا فَاتَّبِعُوهُ ﴾ ١٥٣

And verily, this is my Straight Path, so follow it.[1]

[1] Sūrah al-'An'ām, 6:153

"It is the strong rope," meaning it is the rope which, if the person holds on to it, will save him and guide him to the straight path. Allāh, the Exalted, said:

﴿ وَاعْتَصِمُوا بِحَبْلِ اللَّهِ جَمِيعًا ﴿١٠٣﴾ ﴾

And hold fast, all of you together, to the Rope of Allāh.[1]

"It is the scale," meaning it is what you rely on and judge according to.

﴿ فَإِن تَنَازَعْتُمْ فِي شَيْءٍ فَرُدُّوهُ إِلَى اللَّهِ وَالرَّسُولِ ﴿٥٩﴾ ﴾

If you differ in anything amongst yourselves, refer it to Allāh and His Messenger.[2]

"It is the trustworthy handhold," Allāh, the Exalted, said:

﴿ لَا إِكْرَاهَ فِي الدِّينِ ۖ قَد تَّبَيَّنَ الرُّشْدُ مِنَ الْغَيِّ ۚ فَمَن يَكْفُرْ بِالطَّاغُوتِ
وَيُؤْمِن بِاللَّهِ فَقَدِ اسْتَمْسَكَ بِالْعُرْوَةِ الْوُثْقَىٰ لَا انفِصَامَ لَهَا ﴿٢٥٦﴾ ﴾

There is no compulsion in religion. Verily, the right path has become distinct from the wrong path. Whoever disbelieves in the false deities and believes in Allāh, then he has grasped the most trustworthy handhold that will never break.[3]

---

[1] Sūrah 'Āli 'Imrān, 3:103
[2] Sūrah an-Nisā', 4:59
[3] Sūrah al-Baqarah, 2:256

"For those who adhere to it," whoever desires good for himself that he can adhere to, and good he can hold on to, then hold fast to the Book of Allāh ﷻ; for surely it is the straight path, the strong rope, the just criterion, and the trustworthy handhold.

POEM

هُو البَيَانُ هُو الذِّكْرُ الْحَكِيمُ هُوَ الت تَفْصِيلُ فاقْنَعْ بِهِ فِي كُلِّ مُنْبَهِمِ

It is the clarity, it is the wise reminder, it is the detailed explanation; thus, be content with it as regards to the ambiguous matters.

EXPLANATION

"It is the clarity," meaning it is the clear explanation. The Exalted said:

﴿ هَٰذَا بَيَانٌ لِّلنَّاسِ ﴿١٣٨﴾ ﴾

This (the Qur'an) is a clear statement for mankind.[1]

"It is the wise reminder," the Exalted said:

﴿ إِنَّا نَحْنُ نَزَّلْنَا الذِّكْرَ وَإِنَّا لَهُ لَحَافِظُونَ ﴿٩﴾ ﴾

Indeed, it is We who sent down the Qur'an; and indeed, We will be its guardian.[2]

[1] Sūrah 'Āli 'Imrān, 3:138
[2] Sūrah al-Ḥijr, 15:9

And He ﷻ said:

﴿ذَٰلِكَ نَتْلُوهُ عَلَيْكَ مِنَ الْآيَاتِ وَالذِّكْرِ الْحَكِيمِ ۝٥٨﴾

This is what We recite to you (O Muḥammad) of the Verses and the wise reminder.[1]

"It is the detailed explanation," Allāh, the Exalted, said:

﴿وَمَا كَانَ هَٰذَا الْقُرْآنُ أَن يُفْتَرَىٰ مِن دُونِ اللَّهِ وَلَٰكِن تَصْدِيقَ الَّذِي بَيْنَ يَدَيْهِ وَتَفْصِيلَ الْكِتَابِ ۝٣٧﴾

And this Qur'an is not such as could ever be produced by other than Allāh, but it is a confirmation of (the revelation) that was before it, and a detailed explanation of the Book.[2]

The Exalted said:

﴿مَا كَانَ حَدِيثًا يُفْتَرَىٰ وَلَٰكِن تَصْدِيقَ الَّذِي بَيْنَ يَدَيْهِ وَتَفْصِيلَ كُلِّ شَيْءٍ وَهُدًى وَرَحْمَةً لِّقَوْمٍ يُؤْمِنُونَ ۝١١١﴾

It (the Qur'an) is not a forged statement, but a confirmation of what was before it, and a detailed explanation of all things, and guidance and mercy for a people who believe.[3]

---

[1] Sūrah 'Āli 'Imrān, 3:58
[2] Sūrah Yūnus, 10:37
[3] Sūrah Yūsuf, 12:111

“Thus, be content with it as regards to the ambiguous matters,” the ambiguous matters are everything of which the meaning is hidden from you.

The Qur'an is a Healer for the People of Faith Who Work by It

Poem

هُو البَصائِرُ والذكرَى لِمُدَّكِرٍ هو الْمواعِظُ والبُشْرى لِغَيرِ عَمِي

It is the enlightenment, and the reminder for those who accept the reminder; it is the admonition and lesson, and glad tidings for those who are not blind.

Explanation

"It is the enlightenment," as Allāh, the Exalted, said:

﴿ هَٰذَا بَصَائِرُ لِلنَّاسِ وَهُدًى وَرَحْمَةٌ لِّقَوْمٍ يُوقِنُونَ ﴾

This (Qur'an) is enlightenment for mankind, and guidance and a mercy for people who have Faith with certainty.[1]

[1] Sūrah al-Jāthiyah, 45:20

"And the reminder for those who accept the reminder," as Allāh, the Exalted, said:

﴿ إِنَّ فِي ذَٰلِكَ لَذِكْرَىٰ لِمَن كَانَ لَهُ قَلْبٌ أَوْ أَلْقَى السَّمْعَ وَهُوَ شَهِيدٌ ﴿٣٧﴾ ﴾

Verily, therein is indeed a reminder for him who has a heart or gives ear while he is heedful.[1]

And the Exalted said:

﴿ وَلَقَدْ يَسَّرْنَا الْقُرْآنَ لِلذِّكْرِ فَهَلْ مِن مُّدَّكِرٍ ﴿١٧﴾ ﴾

And We have indeed made the Qur'an easy to understand and remember; then is there any that will remember (or receive admonition)?[2]

"It is the admonition and lesson," Allāh, the Exalted, said:

﴿ هَٰذَا بَيَانٌ لِّلنَّاسِ وَهُدًى وَمَوْعِظَةٌ لِّلْمُتَّقِينَ ﴿١٣٨﴾ ﴾

This (the Qur'an) is a plain statement for mankind, a guidance and instruction to those who are pious.[3]

And the Exalted said:

﴿ يَا أَيُّهَا النَّاسُ قَدْ جَاءَتْكُم مَّوْعِظَةٌ مِّن رَّبِّكُمْ وَشِفَاءٌ لِّمَا فِي الصُّدُورِ وَهُدًى وَرَحْمَةٌ لِّلْمُؤْمِنِينَ ﴿٥٧﴾ ﴾

---

[1] Sūrah Qāf, 50:37

[2] Sūrah al-Qamar, 54:17

[3] Sūrah 'Āli 'Imrān, 3:138

O mankind, there has come to you instruction from your Lord, and healing for what is in the breasts, and guidance and mercy for the believers.[1]

And Allāh, the Exalted, said:

﴿ وَكُلًّا نَّقُصُّ عَلَيْكَ مِنْ أَنبَاءِ الرُّسُلِ مَا نُثَبِّتُ بِهِ فُؤَادَكَ ۚ وَجَاءَكَ فِي هَٰذِهِ الْحَقُّ وَمَوْعِظَةٌ وَذِكْرَىٰ لِلْمُؤْمِنِينَ ﴿١٢٠﴾ ﴾

And all that We relate to you (O Muḥammad) of the news of the Messengers is in order that We may make strong and firm your heart thereby. And in this (Qur'an) has come to you the truth, as well as an admonition and a reminder for the believers.[2]

"And glad tidings for those who are not blind," Allāh, the Exalted, said:

﴿ قُلْ مَن كَانَ عَدُوًّا لِّجِبْرِيلَ فَإِنَّهُ نَزَّلَهُ عَلَىٰ قَلْبِكَ بِإِذْنِ اللَّهِ مُصَدِّقًا لِّمَا بَيْنَ يَدَيْهِ وَهُدًى وَبُشْرَىٰ لِلْمُؤْمِنِينَ ﴿٩٧﴾ ﴾

Say (O Muḥammad): "Whoever is an enemy to Jibrael, then indeed he has brought it (this Qur'an) down to your heart by Allāh's Permission, confirming

[1] Sūrah Yūnus, 10:57
[2] Sūrah Hūd, 11:120

what came before it, and guidance and glad tidings for the believers.[1]

Allāh, the Exalted, said:

﴿ وَمِن قَبْلِهِۦ كِتَٰبُ مُوسَىٰٓ إِمَامًا وَرَحْمَةً ۚ وَهَٰذَا كِتَٰبٌ مُّصَدِّقٌ لِّسَانًا عَرَبِيًّا لِّيُنذِرَ ٱلَّذِينَ ظَلَمُوا۟ وَبُشْرَىٰ لِلْمُحْسِنِينَ ﴿١٢﴾ ﴾

And before this was the Scripture of Mūsā as a guide and a mercy. And this is a confirming Book (the Qur'an) in the Arabic language, to warn those who do wrong, and as glad tidings to the doers of good.[2]

His statement, "for those who are not blind," means those who are not blind from the truth, because he benefits from the enlightenment of the Qur'an; the reminders and lessons it contains, and the glad tidings. The one who is blind from the truth will not benefit from this.

Poem

هُو الْمُنَزَّلُ نُورًا بَيِّنًا وهُدًى وهو الشِّفاءُ لِما فِي الْقَلْبِ مِن سَقَمِ

It was sent down as a clear light and guidancc, and it is a healing for the sickness within the heart.

[1] Sūrah al-Baqarah, 2:97

[2] Sūrah al-'Aḥqāf, 46:12

EXPLANATION

He described the Qur'an as a clear light; meaning a manifest light, as Allāh, the Exalted, said:

﴿ يَا أَيُّهَا النَّاسُ قَدْ جَاءَكُم بُرْهَانٌ مِّن رَّبِّكُمْ وَأَنزَلْنَا إِلَيْكُمْ نُورًا مُّبِينًا ﴿١٧٤﴾ ﴾

O mankind! Verily, there has come to you a convincing proof from your Lord, and We sent down to you a manifest light.[1]

The Exalted said:

﴿ وَكَذَٰلِكَ أَوْحَيْنَا إِلَيْكَ رُوحًا مِّنْ أَمْرِنَا ۚ مَا كُنتَ تَدْرِي مَا الْكِتَابُ وَلَا الْإِيمَانُ وَلَٰكِن جَعَلْنَاهُ نُورًا نَّهْدِي بِهِ مَن نَّشَاءُ مِنْ عِبَادِنَا ۚ وَإِنَّكَ لَتَهْدِي إِلَىٰ صِرَاطٍ مُّسْتَقِيمٍ ﴿٥٢﴾ ﴾

And thus, We have sent to you (O Muḥammad) an inspiration, and a mercy of Our Command. You did not know about the Book nor what is faith. But We have made it (this Qur'an) a light wherewith We guide whosoever of Our slaves We will. And verily, you (O Muḥammad) are indeed guiding (mankind) to the straight path.[2]

---

[1] Sūrah an-Nisā', 4:174

[2] Sūrah ash-Shūraá, 42:52

"Guidance," the Exalted said:

﴿ إِنَّ هَٰذَا الْقُرْآنَ يَهْدِي لِلَّتِي هِيَ أَقْوَمُ وَيُبَشِّرُ الْمُؤْمِنِينَ الَّذِينَ يَعْمَلُونَ الصَّالِحَاتِ أَنَّ لَهُمْ أَجْرًا كَبِيرًا ۝٩ ﴾

Verily, this Qur'an guides to that which is most just and right, and gives glad tidings to the believers who work deeds of righteousness, that they shall have a great reward.[1]

And Allāh, the Exalted, said:

﴿ وَنَزَّلْنَا عَلَيْكَ الْكِتَابَ تِبْيَانًا لِّكُلِّ شَيْءٍ وَهُدًى وَرَحْمَةً وَبُشْرَىٰ لِلْمُسْلِمِينَ ۝٨٩ ﴾

And We have sent down to you the Book (the Qur'an) as an exposition of everything, a guidance, a mercy, and glad tidings for the Muslims.[2]

"And it is a healing for the sickness within the heart," meaning it is a healing for the sicknesses within the heart. Allāh, the Exalted, said:

﴿ يَا أَيُّهَا النَّاسُ قَدْ جَاءَتْكُم مَّوْعِظَةٌ مِّن رَّبِّكُمْ وَشِفَاءٌ لِّمَا فِي الصُّدُورِ وَهُدًى وَرَحْمَةٌ لِّلْمُؤْمِنِينَ ۝٥٧ ﴾

---

[1] Sūrah al-'Isrā', 17:9

[2] Sūrah an-Naḥl, 16:89

O mankind, there has to come to you instruction from your Lord, and healing for what is in the breasts, and guidance and mercy for the believers.[1]

And the Exalted said:

﴿ وَلَوْ جَعَلْنَاهُ قُرْآنًا أَعْجَمِيًّا لَّقَالُوا لَوْلَا فُصِّلَتْ آيَاتُهُ ۖ أَأَعْجَمِيٌّ وَعَرَبِيٌّ ۗ قُلْ هُوَ لِلَّذِينَ آمَنُوا هُدًى وَشِفَاءٌ ﴿٤٤﴾ ﴾

And if We had sent this as a Qur'an in a foreign language other than Arabic, they would have said: "Why are not its Verses explained in detail (in our language)? Is it not in Arabic and (the Messenger) an Arab?" Say: "It is for those who believe, a guide and a healing."[2]

POEM

لَكِنَّهُ لِأُولِي الإِيمانِ إِذْ عَمِلُوا بِما أَتَى فِيه مِنْ عِلْمٍ ومِنْ حِكَمِ

But it is for the people of faith, if they work according to what comes in it from the knowledge and wisdom.

EXPLANATION

The Qur'an is a healing for the people who possess faith, if they work by the knowledge and wisdom contained in it. This brings attention to the healing of the Qur'an, attaining its blessings; and its good is not attained by everyone. It is only attained by the people of faith who work by the

[1] Sūrah Yūnus, 10:57
[2] Sūrah Fuṣṣilat, 41:44

Qur'an. They are the ones who succeed with the blessing of the Qur'an, and the good and healing that it contains. For this reason, Allāh, the Exalted, said:

﴿ وَنُنَزِّلُ مِنَ الْقُرْآنِ مَا هُوَ شِفَاءٌ وَرَحْمَةٌ لِّلْمُؤْمِنِينَ ۙ وَلَا يَزِيدُ الظَّالِمِينَ إِلَّا خَسَارًا ﴿٨٢﴾ ﴾

And We send down from the Qur'an that which is a healing and a mercy to those who believe, and it increases the wrong-doers nothing but loss.[1]

And Allāh, the Exalted, said:

﴿ قُلْ هُوَ لِلَّذِينَ آمَنُوا هُدًى وَشِفَاءٌ ﴿٤٤﴾ ﴾

Say: It is for those who believe, a guide and a healing.[2]

Poem

أمَّا عَلى مَن تَوَلَّى عنه فهو عَمًى لِكَوْنِهِ عَنْ هُداهُ الْمُسْتَنِيرِ عُمِي

Upon the one who turns away from it is blindness, due to him being blind to the enlightened guidance.

[1] Sūrah al-'Isrā', 17:82
[2] Sūrah Fuṣṣilat, 41:44

EXPLANATION

"Upon the one who turns away from it is blindness," this alludes to the statement of the Exalted:

﴿ وَالَّذِينَ لَا يُؤْمِنُونَ فِي آذَانِهِمْ وَقْرٌ وَهُوَ عَلَيْهِمْ عَمًى ﴿٤٤﴾ ﴾

And those who do not believe, in their ears is deafness, and it is upon them blindness.[1]

"Due to him being blind to the enlightened guidance," meaning he turns a blind eye to the clear, evident truth. Thus, he does not have insight to what the Qur'an contains from truth and guidance. This person will not benefit from the healing, goodness and blessings within the Book of Allāh ﷻ.

[1] Sūrah Fuṣṣilat, 41:44

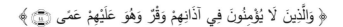

The Promise for Those Who Work by the Qur'an, and the Threat for Those Who Turn Away from It

Poem

فمَنْ يُقِمْهُ يَكُنْ يَومَ الْمَعادِ لَهُ خَيرَ الإمامِ إلَى الفِرْدَوسِ والنِّعَمِ

Those who implement it, on the day of return, for them will be the best guide to the gardens of Paradise and bliss.

Explanation

Those who implement the Qur'an with knowledge and action, Allāh ﷻ will elevate them by the Qur'an and on the Day of Judgement. They will have a leader to guide them to the gardens of Paradise.

Poem:

كمَا يَسُوقُ أولِي الإعْراضِ عنهُ إلَى دارِ الْمَقامِعِ والأنْكالِ والألَمِ

Just those who turn away from it shall be led to the abode of iron hooks, shackles and punishment.

Explanation

Allāh, the Exalted, said:

﴿ وَسِيقَ الَّذِينَ كَفَرُوا إِلَىٰ جَهَنَّمَ زُمَرًا ۖ حَتَّىٰ إِذَا جَاءُوهَا فُتِحَتْ أَبْوَابُهَا وَقَالَ لَهُمْ خَزَنَتُهَا أَلَمْ يَأْتِكُمْ رُسُلٌ مِّنكُمْ يَتْلُونَ عَلَيْكُمْ آيَاتِ رَبِّكُمْ وَيُنذِرُونَكُمْ لِقَاءَ يَوْمِكُمْ هَٰذَا ﴿٧١﴾ ﴾

And those who disbelieved will be driven to Hell in groups, till, when they reach it, the gates thereof will be opened. And its keepers will say, "Did not the Messengers come to you from yourselves, reciting to you the Verses of your Lord, and warning you of the Meeting of this Day of yours?"[1]

And the Exalted said:

﴿ وَمَنْ أَعْرَضَ عَن ذِكْرِي فَإِنَّ لَهُ مَعِيشَةً ضَنكًا وَنَحْشُرُهُ يَوْمَ الْقِيَامَةِ أَعْمَىٰ ﴿١٢٤﴾ ﴾

"But whosoever turns away from My Reminder, verily, for him is a life of hardship, and We shall raise him up blind on the Day of Resurrection."[2]

And Allāh, the Exalted, said:

﴿ وَمَنْ أَظْلَمُ مِمَّن ذُكِّرَ بِآيَاتِ رَبِّهِ ثُمَّ أَعْرَضَ عَنْهَا ۚ إِنَّا مِنَ الْمُجْرِمِينَ مُنتَقِمُونَ ﴿٢٢﴾ ﴾

---

[1] Sūrah az-Zumar, 39:71
[2] Sūrah Ṭāhā, 20:124

And who does more wrong than he who is reminded of the signs of his Lord, then he turns away from them? Verily, We shall exact retribution from the criminals.[1]

Jabir ﷺ said the Prophet ﷺ said:

الْقُرْآن شَافِع مُشَفع وَمَاحِل مُصَدَّقٌ مَنْ جَعَلَهُ إِمَامَهُ قَادَهُ إِلَى الْجَنَّةِ وَمَنْ جَعَلَهُ خَلْفَ ظَهْرِهِ سَاقَهُ إِلَى النَّارِ

"The Qur'an is an intercessor whose intercession will be accepted, and an opponent whose testimony will be accepted. Whoever puts it in front of him, it will lead him to Paradise, and whoever puts it behind his back, it will drive him to Hell."[2]

Abu Mūsā al-'Ash'arī ﷺ said:

إِنَّ هَذَا الْقُرْآنَ كَائِنٌ لَكُمْ ذِكْرَى وَكَائِنٌ لَكُمْ أَجْرًا أَوْ كَانَ عَلَيْكُمْ وِزْرًا ، فَاتَّبِعُوا الْقُرْآنَ وَلَا يَتَّبِعْكُمْ الْقُرْآنُ فَإِنَّهُ مَنْ يَتَّبِعْ الْقُرْآنَ يَهْبِطْ بِهِ عَلَى رِيَاضِ الْجَنَّةِ ، وَمَنْ يَتَّبِعْهُ الْقُرْآنُ يَزُخُّ فِي قَفَاهُ فَيَقْذِفُهُ فِي جَهَنَّمَ

Verily this Qur'an is for you a reminder; and it is for you a reward, or it will be upon you a sin. So follow the Qur'an and do not let the Qur'an follow you. Because whoever follows the Qur'an, it will

[1] Sūrah as-Sajdah, 32:22
[2] Collected by Ibn Ḥibbān, narrated in his collection of *ḥadīth*, 124

land him in the gardens of Paradise, while whoever the Qur'an follows, it will push him in the back of his head and hurl him into the Hellfire.[1]

---

[1] Collected by ibn Abī Shayba, 6/126

The Virtue of Sūrah al-Baqarah and Sūrah 'Āli 'Imrān

Poem

وقَدْ أتَى النصُّ في الطُّولَيْنِ أنَّهُما ظِلٌّ لِتالِيهِما فِي مَوْقِفِ الغَمَمِ

Indeed, there has come in the text, concerning the two long (sūrah), both will be shade for the one who recites them during the standing of distress.

Explanation

He is alluding to the narration collected in Ṣaḥīḥ Muslim, narrated from an-Nawwās ibn Sam'ān ﷺ. He said, I heard the Messenger of Allāh ﷺ say:

" يُؤْتَى بِالْقُرْآنِ يَوْمَ الْقِيَامَةِ وَأَهْلِهِ الَّذِينَ كَانُوا يَعْمَلُونَ بِهِ تَقْدُمُهُ سُورَةُ الْبَقَرَةِ وَآلُ عِمْرَانَ " . وَضَرَبَ لَهُمَا رَسُولُ اللَّهِ صلى الله عليه وسلم ثَلاَثَةَ أَمْثَالٍ مَا نَسِيتُهُنَّ بَعْدُ قَالَ " كَأَنَّهُمَا غَمَامَتَانِ أَوْ ظُلَّتَانِ سَوْدَاوَانِ بَيْنَهُمَا شَرْقٌ أَوْ كَأَنَّهُمَا حِزْقَانِ مِنْ طَيْرٍ صَوَافَّ تُحَاجَّانِ عَنْ صَاحِبِهِمَا

The Qur'an will be brought forward on the Day of Resurrection, and those who acted accordingly will be brought with Sūrah al-Baqarah and Sūrah 'Āli 'Imrān preceding them. The Messenger of Allāh ﷺ likened them to three things, which I did not forget afterwards. He likened them to two clouds, or two black shadows with light and radiance between them, or like two flocks of birds in ranks; pleading for one who recited them.[1]

Poem

وأنَّه فِي غَدٍ يَأْتِي لِصاحِبِهِ مُبَشِّرًا وحَجِيجًا عَنْهُ إنْ يَقُمِ

والْمُلْكَ والْخُلْدَ يُعْطِيهِ ويُلْبِسُهُ تاجَ الوَقارِ الإلهُ الْحَقُّ ذو الكَرَمِ

يُقالُ إقْرَأْ ورَتِّلْ وارْقَ فِي غُرَفِ الْ جَناتِ كَيْ تَنْتَهِي لِلْمَنْزِلِ النَّعِمِ

وحُلَّتانِ مِن الفِرْدَوسِ قَدْ كُسِيَتْ لِوالِدَيْهِ لَها الأكْوانُ لَمْ تَقُمِ

قالَا بِماذا كُسِيناهَا فقيلَ بِما أقْرَأْتُمَا ابْنَكُما فاشْكُرْ لِذِي النِّعَمِ

Indeed, tomorrow they will come with their companion, with glad tidings and arguing on his behalf, if he implemented.

The dominion and eternity will be given to him, and he will be crowned with the crown of dignity, the true God is generous.

---

[1] Ṣaḥīḥ Muslim, 805

It will be said 'recite, and be methodical in your recitation, and ascend to the lofty rooms of Paradise so you may reach the homes of bliss.

Two garments from the lofty gardens of Paradise, which will adorn his parents the like of which the worlds could not produce.

His parents will say, "What allowed us to be adorned with this?" It will be said, "By the recitation of your children. Thus, show gratitude to the Owner of blessings."

EXPLANATION

"If he implemented," means if he implemented the Glorious Qur'an with knowledge and action.

"The dominion and eternity will be given to him," meaning he will be given the dominion in his right hand and eternity in his left hand. These two blessings combine the bliss of the Hereafter.

"He will be crowned with the crown of dignity," the crown is what is formed for the kings from gold and jewels.

These five lines of poetry allude to what is mentioned in the *ḥadīth* of Buraida ibn al-Ḥasīb ﷺ. He said:

كُنْتُ جَالِسًا عِنْدَ النَّبِيِّ صَلَّى اللَّهُ عَلَيْهِ وَسَلَّمَ فَسَمِعْتُهُ يَقُولُ : تَعَلَّمُوا سُورَةَ الْبَقَرَةِ ، فَإِنَّ أَخْذَهَا بَرَكَةٌ ، وَتَرْكَهَا حَسْرَةٌ ، وَلَا تَسْتَطِيعُهَا الْبَطَلَةُ . قَالَ : ثُمَّ سَكَتَ سَاعَةً ، ثُمَّ قَالَ : تَعَلَّمُوا سُورَةَ الْبَقَرَةِ ، وَآلَ عِمْرَانَ ، فَإِنَّهُمَا الزَّهْرَاوَانِ ، يُظِلَّانِ صَاحِبَهُمَا يَوْمَ الْقِيَامَةِ ،

كَأَنَّهُمَا غَمَامَتَانِ أَوْ غَيَايَتَانِ ، أَوْ فِرْقَانِ مِنْ طَيْرٍ صَوَافَّ ، وَإِنَّ الْقُرْآنَ يَلْقَى صَاحِبَهُ يَوْمَ الْقِيَامَةِ حِينَ يَنْشَقُّ عَنْهُ قَبْرُهُ كَالرَّجُلِ الشَّاحِبِ ، فَيَقُولُ لَهُ : هَلْ تَعْرِفُنِي ؟ فَيَقُولُ : مَا أَعْرِفُكَ . فَيَقُولُ : أَنَا صَاحِبُكَ الْقُرْآنُ الَّذِي أَظْمَأْتُكَ فِي الْهَوَاجِرِ ، وَأَسْهَرْتُ لَيْلَكَ ، وَإِنَّ كُلَّ تَاجِرٍ مِنْ وَرَاءِ تِجَارَتِهِ ، وَإِنَّكَ الْيَوْمَ مِنْ وَرَاءِ كُلِّ تِجَارَةٍ . فَيُعْطَى الْمُلْكَ بِيَمِينِهِ وَالْخُلْدَ بِشِمَالِهِ ، وَيُوضَعُ عَلَى رَأْسِهِ تَاجُ الْوَقَارِ ، وَيُكْسَى وَالِدَاهُ حُلَّتَيْنِ ، لَا يَقُومُ لَهُمَا أَهْلُ الدُّنْيَا ، فَيَقُولَانِ : بِمَ كُسِينَا هَذَا ؟ فَيُقَالُ : بِأَخْذِ وَلَدِكُمَا الْقُرْآنَ ، ثُمَّ يُقَالُ : اقْرَأْ وَاصْعَدْ فِي دَرَجِ الْجَنَّةِ وَغُرَفِهَا ، فَهُوَ فِي صُعُودٍ مَا دَامَ يَقْرَأُ هَذًّا كَانَ أَوْ تَرْتِيلًا

We were sitting with the Prophet ﷺ and I heard him saying: "Learn Sūrah al-Baqarah, for adhering to it is blessing and abandoning it is loss; and magicians cannot confront it." Then he was silent for a moment, and he said: "Learn Sūrah al-Baqarah and Sūrah 'Āli 'Imrān, for surely they are two lights that will shade its companion on the Day of Judgment; as though they are two clouds, or two shades, or two flocks of birds spreading their wings. The Qur'an will come to its companion when his grave is split open as a pale man. It will say to him, 'Do you recognize me?' The person will say, 'I do not recognize you.' It will say, 'I am your companion, the Qur'an that kept you thirsty during the day and kept you awake at night.' Every merchant is behind his merchandise, and indeed today you are behind your merchandise. Thus, he will be given his dominion in his right hand and eternity in his left hand, and the crown of dignity will be placed on his head. His parents will be adorned in garments the likes of which the inhabitants of the world could not produce. They will say, 'How did we get dressed in this?' It will be said, 'By your children taking hold of the Qur'an.' Then it will be

said: 'Recite and ascend in levels in Paradise and the lofty rooms.' Thus, he will continue to ascend as long as he recites.[1]

---

[1] Collected by Aḥmad, 1190

The Qur'an is a Continuous Miracle

Poem

كَفَى وحَسْبُكَ بالقُرْآنِ مُعْجِزَةً دامَتْ لَدَيْنَا دومًا غيْرَ مُنْصَرِمِ

لَمْ يَعْتَرِهْ قطُّ تَبْدِيلٌ ولا غِيَرٌ وَجَلَّ فِي كَثْرَةِ التَّرْدادِ عنْ سَأَمِ

Sufficient for you is the Qur'an as a continuous miracle, always with us, never departed.

Alteration has never shaken it nor has change, and it is too great for its numerous repeat recitations to cause boredom.

Explanation

The miracle of the Qur'an is sufficient for you, as it is the greatest of all miracles.

"Never departed," means it never ceases; rather, it is a continuous miracle. Ibn al-Qayyim said in his book, *Supporting the Distressed*, after mentioning the miracles of Prophets Mūsā and Jesus peace be upon them, "If this is the status of the miracles of these two Messengers (meaning Mūsā and

Jesus peace be upon them)—despite the long time which has passed, the dismantling of the unity of their nations throughout the earth, and their miracles ceasing to exists—then what do you think about the prophecy of the one whose miracles and signs exceed one thousand in number![1] His era is more recent than their era. His miracles were transmitted by the most truthful and pious of the creation. It has been transmitted through numerous reliable chains of transmission, generation after generation. The greatest of these miracles is the remaining Book, fresh and unsullied; nothing from it has been changed or altered. Rather it is as though it was sent down at this very moment. It is the Glorious Qur'an. The events mentioned in it occur just as they are mentioned, as though it is an eye witness of what occurs."

"Nor has change," Allāh, the Exalted, said:

﴿ إِنَّا نَحْنُ نَزَّلْنَا الذِّكْرَ وَإِنَّا لَهُ لَحَافِظُونَ ﴿٩﴾ ﴾

Verily, it is We Who have sent down the Reminder (the Qur'an) and surely, We will guard it.[2]

Ibn al-Qayyim, ﷺ said in his book, *Clarifying the Oaths in the Qur'an*[3], "Allāh ﷻ protected it from increase, decrease or alteration. He protected its meanings from being distorted, just as He protected it words from alteration. He established people who memorized it letters without increase or decrease, and its meanings without distortion or change."

---

[1] Translator's note: Imam Nawawī said in his introduction to the explanation of Ṣaḥīḥ Muslim that the miracles of the Prophet ﷺ exceed 1,200 miracles.

[2] Sūrah al-Ḥijr, 15:9

[3] *Clarifying the Oaths in the Qur'an*, 2/100

"It is too great for its numerous repeat recitation to cause boredom," meaning the one who recites the Qur'an and repeats its recitation will not become bored, despite the numerous times he recites it. It has been narrated that 'Alī ﷺ said, I heard the Messenger of Allāh ﷺ saying:

أَلاَ إِنَّهَا سَتَكُونُ فِتْنَةٌ " . فَقُلْتُ مَا الْمَخْرَجُ مِنْهَا يَا رَسُولَ اللَّهِ قَالَ " كِتَابُ اللَّهِ فِيهِ نَبَأُ مَا كَانَ قَبْلَكُمْ وَخَبَرُ مَا بَعْدَكُمْ وَحُكْمُ مَا بَيْنَكُمْ هُوَ الْفَصْلُ لَيْسَ بِالْهَزْلِ مَنْ تَرَكَهُ مِنْ جَبَّارٍ قَصَمَهُ اللَّهُ وَمَنِ ابْتَغَى الْهُدَى فِي غَيْرِهِ أَضَلَّهُ اللَّهُ وَهُوَ حَبْلُ اللَّهِ الْمَتِينُ وَهُوَ الذِّكْرُ الْحَكِيمُ وَهُوَ الصِّرَاطُ الْمُسْتَقِيمُ هُوَ الَّذِي لاَ تَزِيغُ بِهِ الأَهْوَاءُ وَلاَ تَلْتَبِسُ بِهِ الأَلْسِنَةُ وَلاَ يَشْبَعُ مِنْهُ الْعُلَمَاءُ وَلاَ يَخْلَقُ عَلَى كَثْرَةِ الرَّدِّ وَلاَ تَنْقَضِي عَجَائِبُهُ هُوَ الَّذِي لَمْ تَنْتَهِ الْجِنُّ إِذْ سَمِعَتْهُ حَتَّى قَالُوا (إِنَّا سَمِعْنَا قُرْآنًا عَجَبًا * يَهْدِي إِلَى الرُّشْدِ) مَنْ قَالَ بِهِ صَدَقَ وَمَنْ عَمِلَ بِهِ أُجِرَ وَمَنْ حَكَمَ بِهِ عَدَلَ وَمَنْ دَعَا إِلَيْهِ هُدِيَ إِلَى صِرَاطٍ مُسْتَقِيمٍ

"Indeed, there comes a fitnah." So I said, "What is the way out from it, O Messenger of Allāh?" He said, "The Book of Allāh. In it is news for what happened before you, and information about what comes after you, and judgement for what happens between you. It is the criterion, it is not jest and amusement. Whoever among the oppressive abandons it, Allāh will break him, and whoever seeks guidance from other than it, then Allāh will lead him astray. It is the firm rope of Allāh, it is the wise remembrance, it is the straight path, and it is that which the desires cannot mislead, nor can the tongues distort it, nor can the scholars ever have enough of it, and it does not become dull from reciting it much, and the amazement of it does not diminish. It is the one that when the *jinn* heard it, they did not hesitate to say about it, 'Verily, we have heard a wonderful Recitation! It guides to the Right Path, and we have believed

therein.' Whoever speaks according to it, then he spoke the truth; and whoever acts according to it, he is rewarded; and whoever judges by it, he has judged justly; and whoever invites to it, then he guides to the straight path."[1]

Imam Tirmidhī declared this narration as weak with his statement, "This *ḥadīth* is *gharīb*[2]." We only know it from this angle, and its chain is weak; and then there are statements concerning al-Ḥarith (one of the narrators).

However, the meaning of this *ḥadīth* is authentic, and everything mentioned in it is the truth. But it has not been authenticated from the Prophet ﷺ.

---

[1] Collected by Tirmidhī, 2906

[2] Translator's note: Shaykh bin Baz said the *ḥadīth* is called "*gharīb*" (strange) if it only has one chain of narration. If the people in the chain are reliable, the *ḥadīth* is authentic, even if it is *gharīb*; thus, we implement the *ḥadīth*. But if someone in the chain of narration is weak, then the *ḥadīth* is weak and is not implemented.

The Qur’an is a Superior Witness

Poem

مُهَيْمِنًا عَرَبِيًّا غيرَ ذِي عِوَجٍ مُصَدِّقًا جاءَ فِي التَّنْزِيلِ فِي القِدَمِ

It is a superior witness in the Arabic language, with no crookedness, affirming what came in the scriptures from before.

Explanation

“It is a superior witness,” the word *muhaiminan* means it has superiority over the Books which came before it. As Allāh, the Exalted, said:

﴿ وَأَنزَلْنَا إِلَيْكَ الْكِتَابَ بِالْحَقِّ مُصَدِّقًا لِّمَا بَيْنَ يَدَيْهِ مِنَ الْكِتَابِ وَمُهَيْمِنًا عَلَيْهِ ﴿٤٨﴾ ﴾

And We have revealed to you, (O Muḥammad), the Book in truth, confirming that which preceded it of the Scripture, and as a criterion over it.[1]

---

[1] Sūrah al-Mā'idah, 5:48

Concerning the statement "a criterion over it," Ibn Kathīr said, "Sufyān ath-Thawrī, and others, have narrated from Abu Isḥaq at-Tamimi, from Ibn 'Abbas, that he said this word, *muhaiminan*, means 'trustworthy'. And he said, 'The Qur'an is the guardian over all previous Books.' Ibn Jarir said, 'The Qur'an is the guardian over the previous Books; therefore, what agrees with the Qur'an is the truth, and what contradicts it is false.' Ibn 'Abbas also said this word means a witness and judge over the previous Books. All of these meanings are similar, and this word comprises all these meanings. The Qur'an is a trustworthy witness and judge over the previous Books. Allāh ﷻ made it such that this Great Book, that was sent as the final Book and seal of the Books, is the most complete and greatest; such that it contains all the good from the previous Books, while having extra that is not found in the previous Books. For this reason, He ﷻ made it such that this Book is the witness, criterion and judge over the previous Books."

"In the Arabic language," as Allāh, the Exalted, said:

﴿ إِنَّا أَنزَلْنَاهُ قُرْآنًا عَرَبِيًّا لَّعَلَّكُمْ تَعْقِلُونَ ﴿٢﴾ ﴾

Verily, We have sent it down as an Arabic Qur'an, in order that you may understand.[1]

And the Exalted said:

﴿ وَكَذَٰلِكَ أَنزَلْنَاهُ قُرْآنًا عَرَبِيًّا وَصَرَّفْنَا فِيهِ مِنَ الْوَعِيدِ لَعَلَّهُمْ يَتَّقُونَ أَوْ يُحْدِثُ لَهُمْ ذِكْرًا ﴿١١٣﴾ ﴾

[1] Sūrah Yūsuf, 12:2

And thus, We have sent it down as a Qur'an in Arabic, and have explained therein in detail the warnings, in order that they may fear Allāh, or that it may cause them to have a lesson from it.[1]

"With no crookedness," as Allāh, the Exalted, said:

﴿ قُرْآنًا عَرَبِيًّا غَيْرَ ذِي عِوَجٍ لَّعَلَّهُمْ يَتَّقُونَ ﴿٢٨﴾ ﴾

An Arabic Qur'an, without any crookedness (therein), in order that they may avoid all evil which Allāh has ordered them to avoid, fear Him and keep their duty to Him.[2]

﴿ الْحَمْدُ لِلَّهِ الَّذِي أَنزَلَ عَلَىٰ عَبْدِهِ الْكِتَابَ وَلَمْ يَجْعَل لَّهُ عِوَجًا ﴿١﴾ ﴾

All the praises and thanks be to Allāh, Who has sent down to His slave the Book, and has not placed therein any crookedness.[3]

"Affirming what came in the scriptures from before," as Allāh, the Exalted, said:

﴿ وَآمِنُوا بِمَا أَنزَلْتُ مُصَدِّقًا لِّمَا مَعَكُمْ ﴿٤١﴾ ﴾

---

[1] Sūrah Ṭāhā, 20:113
[2] Sūrah az-Zumar, 39:28
[3] Sūrah al-Kahf, 18:1

And believe in what I have sent down (this Qur'an), confirming that which is with you.[1]

And the Exalted said:

﴿ وَإِذَا قِيلَ لَهُمْ آمِنُوا بِمَا أَنزَلَ اللَّهُ قَالُوا نُؤْمِنُ بِمَا أُنزِلَ عَلَيْنَا
وَيَكْفُرُونَ بِمَا وَرَاءَهُ وَهُوَ الْحَقُّ مُصَدِّقًا لِّمَا مَعَهُمْ ﴿٩١﴾ ﴾

And when it is said to them (the Jews), "Believe in what Allāh has sent down," they say, "We believe in what was sent down to us." And they disbelieve in that which came after it, while it is the truth, confirming what is with them.[2]

The Exalted said:

﴿ نَزَّلَ عَلَيْكَ الْكِتَابَ بِالْحَقِّ مُصَدِّقًا لِّمَا بَيْنَ يَدَيْهِ وَأَنزَلَ التَّوْرَاةَ
وَالْإِنجِيلَ ﴿٣﴾ ﴾

It is He Who has sent down the Book (the Qur'an) to you (Muḥammad) with truth, confirming what came before it. And he sent down the Torah and the Injīl.[3]

---

[1] Sūrah al-Baqarah, 2:41
[2] Sūrah al-Baqarah, 2:91
[3] Sūrah 'Āli 'Imrān, 3:3

The Qur'an Contains Laws and Information of Past Nations

Poem

فيهِ التفاصِيلُ للأحْكامِ مَعْ نَبَأٍ عمَّا سَيأتِي وعنْ ماضٍ مِن الأمَمِ

In it are detailed laws and regulations, along with information about future events and past nations.

Explanation

"In it are detailed laws and regulations," meaning the Noble Qur'an contains detailed legislative rulings, clarification of the permissible and impermissible, the commands and prohibitions, the obligations, recommended acts and hated acts. All of this is explained in detail in the Book of Allāh ﷻ. As Allāh, the Exalted, said:

﴿ مَا كَانَ حَدِيثًا يُفْتَرَىٰ وَلَٰكِن تَصْدِيقَ الَّذِي بَيْنَ يَدَيْهِ وَتَفْصِيلَ كُلِّ شَيْءٍ وَهُدًى وَرَحْمَةً لِّقَوْمٍ يُؤْمِنُونَ ﴿١١١﴾ ﴾

It (the Qur'an) is not a forged statement, but a confirmation of Allāh's existing Books; and a detailed

explanation of everything, and a guide and a mercy for the people who believe.[1]

He ﷻ said to His Prophet ﷺ:

﴿ وَكَذَٰلِكَ أَوْحَيْنَا إِلَيْكَ رُوحًا مِّنْ أَمْرِنَا ۚ مَا كُنتَ تَدْرِي مَا الْكِتَابُ وَلَا الْإِيمَانُ وَلَٰكِن جَعَلْنَاهُ نُورًا نَّهْدِي بِهِ مَن نَّشَاءُ مِنْ عِبَادِنَا ﴿٥٢﴾ ﴾

And thus, We have sent to you (O Muḥammad) an inspiration, and a mercy of Our Command. You did not know about the Book, nor what is faith. But We have made it (this Qur'an) a light wherewith We guide whosoever of Our slaves.[2]

His ﷻ statement, "You did not know about the Book, nor what is faith," means he ﷺ did not know about the details of the legislation until the clarification came in the noble revelation and wise reminder.

"Along with information about future events and past nations," meaning in addition to the Qur'an containing rules and regulations, it contains information about the earliest nations, and stories about people from the past. It also contains stories of what will occur to future nations. In the previously mentioned *ḥadīth* from 'Alī ibn Abī Ṭālib, he said, "The Book of Allāh ﷻ, in it is news for what happened before you, and information about what comes after you, and judgement for what happens between you." These three affairs are what the poet mentioned in this section of the poem.

[1] Sūrah Yūsuf, 12:111
[2] Sūrah ash-Shūrā, 42:52

POEM

فانْظُرْ قَوارِعَ آياتِ الْمَعادِ بِهِ وانْظُرْ لِما قَصَّ عَنْ عادٍ وعَنْ إرَمِ

Look at the verses concerning the calamity on the Day of Return, and look at what has been narrated about ʻAad and 'Iram.

EXPLANATION

"Look at the verses concerning the calamity on the Day of Return," meaning look and ponder over the verses about what will occur on the Day of Return, and the details of the Day of Judgment, and the terror, horror and distress on that day. Also, ponder over what is connected to the return, the resurrection, the gathering, the reward, punishment Paradise and Hellfire.

"Look at what has been narrated about ʻAad and 'Iram," also look in the Qur'an concerning the stories of the rebellious nations, how Allāh ﷻ permitted various types of punishments upon them. All of this is detailed in numerous places in the Book of Allāh, the Exalted. Like the statement of the Exalted:

﴿أَلَمْ تَرَ كَيْفَ فَعَلَ رَبُّكَ بِعَادٍ ۝٦ إِرَمَ ذَاتِ الْعِمَادِ ۝٧ الَّتِي لَمْ يُخْلَقْ مِثْلُهَا فِي الْبِلَادِ ۝٨ وَثَمُودَ الَّذِينَ جَابُوا الصَّخْرَ بِالْوَادِ ۝٩ وَفِرْعَوْنَ ذِي الْأَوْتَادِ ۝١٠ الَّذِينَ طَغَوْا فِي الْبِلَادِ ۝١١ فَأَكْثَرُوا فِيهَا الْفَسَادَ ۝١٢ فَصَبَّ عَلَيْهِمْ رَبُّكَ سَوْطَ عَذَابٍ ۝١٣ إِنَّ رَبَّكَ لَبِالْمِرْصَادِ ۝١٤﴾

Have you not considered how your Lord dealt with ʻAad, 'Iram, who were very tall like lofty pillars, the like of which were not created in the land; and

Thamūd, who carved out the rocks in the valley; and Pharaoh, owner of the stakes; all of whom oppressed within the lands, and made therein much mischief. So your Lord poured on them different kinds of severe torment. Verily, your Lord is Ever Watchful.[1]

'Aad is another name for 'Iram, a well-known tribe that was in Yemen.

[1] Sūrah al-Fajr, 89:6-14

The Qur'an Explains the Legislative Rulings in a Clear, Easy Method

Poem

وانْظُرْ بهِ شَرْحَ أحْكامِ الشَّريعَةِ هلْ تَرى بِها مِن عَويصٍ غيرِ مُنْفَصِمِ

Look at the explanation of the rules of the legislation, do you see in it anything difficult unresolved?

Explanation

Look in the Qur'an, at the explanation of the rules of the legislation; and you will find it clear and detailed in the most complete manner.

"Do you see in it anything difficult unresolved," meaning ponder over the laws and regulations that appear in the Qur'an. Do you see any laws that are difficult, whether this difficulty is in the understanding, action or implementation? And if it happens that you find something that is problematic to certain individuals, then is there anything in the legislation that goes unresolved and is never clarified? Or is it a legislation that is clear, with easy affairs?

The Qur'an Calls to Everything Good and Prevents Everything Evil

Poem

أمْ مِن صَلاحٍ ولَمْ يَهْدِ الأنامَ لَهُ أمْ بابُ هلْكٍ ولَمْ يَزْجُرْ ولَمْ يَلُمِ

Or is there some good which it does not guide the creation to, or a door of destruction it does not prevent or blame?

Explanation

"The creation," here, refers to mankind and *jinn* because these two groups are addressed with the guidance of the Noble Qur'an.

The meaning of this line of poetry is: when you ponder the text of the Qur'an, do you see any benefits or good for the slaves of Allāh ﷻ—which contains happiness in this world and the Hereafter—that it does not guide the creation to? Or are there, in the Qur'an, any affairs which result in destruction, corruption or harm upon the creation that it does not prevent or warn against?

Ibn Taymiyyah رحمه الله explained the completeness of the legislation of Islam for all good, and guidance to rectification and happiness; while preventing all evil and falsehood. He said in his collection of Islamic verdicts, "Allāh ﷻ commanded His Messenger ﷺ with every good and prohibited every evil. He permitted all good things and prohibited all filthy things. It has been authentically narrated from him that he ﷺ said:

إِنَّهُ لَمْ يَكُنْ نَبِيٌّ قَبْلِي إِلَّا كَانَ حَقًّا عَلَيْهِ أَنْ يَدُلَّ أُمَّتَهُ عَلَى خَيْرِ مَا يَعْلَمُهُ لَهُمْ ، وَيُنْذِرَهُمْ
شَرَّ مَا يَعْلَمُهُ لَهُمْ

There has never been a Prophet before me except that it was incumbent upon him to direct his nation to the good he knew for them, and to warn them against the evil he knew for them.[1]

It must be known that the righteous actions, Allāh ﷻ has commanded them either as an obligation or recommendation; while Allāh ﷻ has prohibited the evil deeds. If a deed contains both good and evil, and the good outweighs the evil, it is allowed. But if the evil outweighs the good, then it is not allowed, rather it is prohibited. As Allāh, the Exalted, said:

﴿ كُتِبَ عَلَيْكُمُ الْقِتَالُ وَهُوَ كُرْهٌ لَّكُمْ ۖ وَعَسَىٰ أَن تَكْرَهُوا شَيْئًا وَهُوَ
خَيْرٌ لَّكُمْ ۖ وَعَسَىٰ أَن تُحِبُّوا شَيْئًا وَهُوَ شَرٌّ لَّكُمْ ۗ وَاللَّهُ يَعْلَمُ وَأَنتُمْ لَا
تَعْلَمُونَ ﴿٢١٦﴾ ﴾

Fighting is ordained for you (Muslims) though you dislike it, and it may be that you dislike a thing

[1] Muslim, 1844

which is good for you, and that you like a thing which is bad for you. Allāh knows but you do not know.[1]

And the Exalted said:

﴿ يَسْأَلُونَكَ عَنِ الْخَمْرِ وَالْمَيْسِرِ ۖ قُلْ فِيهِمَا إِثْمٌ كَبِيرٌ وَمَنَافِعُ لِلنَّاسِ وَإِثْمُهُمَا أَكْبَرُ مِن نَّفْعِهِمَا ﴿٢١٩﴾ ﴾

They ask you (O Muḥammad) concerning alcoholic drink and gambling. Say, "In them is a great sin, and (some) benefit for men, but the sin of them is greater than their benefit."[2]

For this reason, Allāh ﷻ prohibited alcohol and gambling. Likewise, the actions that the people believe will bring them closer to Allāh, but Allāh and His Messenger ﷺ did not legislate, then it is a must that the harm is greater than the benefit; because if the benefit was greater than the harm, the legislation would not have neglected it. Allāh ﷻ is All-Wise, He does not neglect benefit in the religion, or that which would bring the believers closer to the Lord of all that exists."[3]

Ibn Taymiyyah also said, "The Islamic legislation comes to bring the benefits and complete it, and it comes to negate the evil and minimize it. Otherwise, all things that are impermissible—to include polytheism, alcohol, gambling, lewdness and oppression—bring about benefit and the desired goal of the person who participates in these actions. But

---

[1] Sūrah al-Baqarah, 2:216
[2] Sūrah al-Baqarah, 2:219
[3] Collection of religious verdicts, 11/623-624

because the evil of these actions outweighs the good, Allāh ﷻ and His Messenger ﷺ have prohibited them. Just as there are many affairs such as acts of worship, *jihad* and spending wealth in charity that could cause some harm, but because the benefit overcomes the harm the legislation commanded it.[1]

[1] Collection of religious verdicts, 1/265

Manmade Laws Are Not Independent of Needing the Guidance of the Qur'an

Poem

أمْ كانَ يُغْنِي نَقِيرًا عن هِدايَتِهِ جَميعُ ما عندَ أهلِ الأرضِ مِنْ نُظُمِ

Or is there equivalent to a date kernel that which is in no need of its guidance due to all the systems from inhabitants of the earths.

Explanation

The *naqīra* refers to the small dot on the back of the date kernel. It is not possible that man is in no need of the Qur'an, because the Islamic legislation came with all good; and it guides to all rectification and success. Thus, it is not possible that the systems and laws invented by man—that sprouted from his intellect and ideology—can make man independent of needing the Qur'an.

The meaning of this line of poetry is: Is anyone independent of needing the guidance of the Qur'an; even the amount of a date kernel or the smallest amount, due to the manmade laws the people have devised from our intellects and thoughts?! The answer is no; because the legislation of Allāh

ﷺ came complete with each and every good, success and happiness for the people in this life and the Hereafter.

Ibn al Qayyim's Statement on Relying Solely on the Islamic Legislation

Ibn al-Qayyim ﷺ said in the closing of his book, *I'lam al-Muwaqqi'īn*, "This principle is from the most important and beneficial principles. It is the generality of his message ﷺ as it relates to everything needed by the people in their knowledge, sciences and actions. The *'ummah* has no need of anyone after him. Their only need is for the One the Prophet ﷺ conveyed from (meaning Allāh ﷻ), along with what the Prophet ﷺ conveyed to them. His message is universal and protected. It is universal in regard to whom the message was sent to, and it is universal in regard to containing everything they require from the foundational and subsidiary matters of the religion. Thus, his message is complete, sufficient and universal. There is no need for anything else. Believing in the Prophet ﷺ is not complete without affirming that his message is universal in these matters. There is no one who is independent and outside the scope of his message. And there is no category of truth that is needed by the *'ummah*, in their knowledge or actions, that is outside the scope of his message.

Before the Messenger of Allāh ﷺ died, there was not a bird flying in the sky with his wings except that he mentioned to his *'ummah* some knowledge about it. He ﷺ taught them everything; even the manners of relieving oneself in the bathroom, intimacy, sleeping, waking up, standing, sitting, eating, drinking, riding, settling in an area, travelling, residency, silence, speech, isolation, mingling, prosperity, poverty, health, and sickness. He taught us all the aspects of life and death. He ﷺ described to the *'ummah* the throne of Allāh ﷻ, and His footstool; the angels, *jinn*, Hellfire, and Paradise. He ﷺ described the Day of Judgement, and what will occur on that day, as though he was an eye witness to it.

He ﷺ taught them about the One they worship, their God ﷻ, with complete knowledge; such that it is as though they see Him and witness Him through His complete and perfect attributes and lofty descriptions.

He ﷺ taught them about the prophets, the nations of the prophets and what occurred to them; such that it is as though they lived amongst them. He ﷺ taught them the paths of good and evil in a detailed precise manner, in a way no prophet before him had done. He ﷺ taught them the events surrounding death; and what will happen in the realm between life and death, and the bliss and punishment that occur to the soul and body in a manner which no Prophet had taught before him. Likewise, he ﷺ taught them the evidence of *tawḥīd*, prophecy and the refutation upon all the sects of disbelief and misguidance; such that the one who knows what he taught is not in need of anyone after him. Their only need for his knowledge to be conveyed and explained to them. He ﷺ taught them the schemes of war and encountering the enemy; the means of victory, such that if they know it, understand it and give it its proper attention and concern, the enemy can never gain mastery over them.

He ﷺ taught them about the plots of 'Iblīs and the many paths by which he comes to them. He ﷺ taught them to be on guard against his plots and schemes, and what will protect them from his evil; such that nothing can be added to what he taught.

He ﷺ taught them the conditions of the soul, its attributes, its machinations and traps; such that nothing more is required.

He ﷺ taught them the means of livelihood; such that if they know it and implement it, they will establish their worldly life in the most excellent manner.

In summary; he ﷺ came to them with the good of this world and the Hereafter, in its entirety. Allāh ﷻ did not give them a need for anyone else. So how can anyone believe—having never seen such a complete legislation—that there is a more complete legislation from these incomplete laws which require independent politics to complete it, or deductive reasoning and intellect to complete it?!

Whoever believes this is like the one who believes the people need another messenger after him ﷺ. The reason for this mindset is their unawareness of what he came with, their scant understanding of what Allāh ﷻ blessed the companions of the Prophet ﷺ with. Those companions who sufficed with what the Prophet ﷺ came with and did not look toward anything else. By way of this, they conquered hearts and land. 'Umar رضي الله عنه used to prevent the people from the *ḥadīth* of the Messenger of Allāh ﷺ, fearing it would distract them from the Qur'an. So, what if he saw the people busy and distracted with their opinions, their shallow ideologies, and the rubbish of their minds, from the Qur'an and the *ḥadīth*?! And with Allāh ﷻ aid is sought.[1]

[1] I'lam al-Muwaqqi'in, 4/377

The Qur'an Contains Admonitions and Lessons

Poem

أخبارُهُ عِظَةٌ أمثالُه عِبَرٌ وكُلُّهُ عَجَبٌ سُحْقًا لِذِي صَمَمِ

Its news is an admonition, its examples are lessons;
all of it is amazing, distancing those who are deaf.

Explanation

The news of the Qur'an is an admonition for those who accept warnings. Allāh, the Exalted, said:

﴿ هَٰذَا بَيَانٌ لِّلنَّاسِ وَهُدًى وَمَوْعِظَةٌ لِّلْمُتَّقِينَ ﴿١٣٨﴾ ﴾

This (the Qur'an) is a plain statement for mankind,
a guidance and instruction to those who are pious.[1]

---

[1] Sūrah 'Āli 'Imrān, 3:138

And the Exalted said:

﴿ يَا أَيُّهَا النَّاسُ قَدْ جَاءَتْكُم مَّوْعِظَةٌ مِّن رَّبِّكُمْ وَشِفَاءٌ لِّمَا فِي الصُّدُورِ وَهُدًى وَرَحْمَةٌ لِّلْمُؤْمِنِينَ ﴿٥٧﴾ ﴾

O mankind, there has to come to you instruction from your Lord, and healing for what is in the breasts, and guidance and mercy for the believers.[1]

Those who look at the stories of the Qur'an will find in them warnings and lessons.

﴿ لَقَدْ كَانَ فِي قَصَصِهِمْ عِبْرَةٌ لِّأُولِي الْأَلْبَابِ ﴿١١١﴾ ﴾

Indeed, in their stories, there is a lesson for people of understanding.[2]

"Its examples are lessons," meaning it is a lesson for those who have understanding. Allāh, the Exalted, said:

﴿ وَتِلْكَ الْأَمْثَالُ نَضْرِبُهَا لِلنَّاسِ ۖ وَمَا يَعْقِلُهَا إِلَّا الْعَالِمُونَ ﴿٤٣﴾ ﴾

And these similitudes We put forward for mankind, but none will understand them except those who have knowledge.[3]

---

[1] Sūrah Yūnus, 10:57
[2] Sūrah Yūsuf, 12:111
[3] Sūrah al-'Ankabūt, 29:43

And He said:

﴿ وَتِلْكَ الْأَمْثَالُ نَضْرِبُهَا لِلنَّاسِ لَعَلَّهُمْ يَتَفَكَّرُونَ ﴾

Such are the parables which We put forward to mankind, that they may reflect.[1]

"All of it is amazing," meaning all of the Qur'an is amazing. As Allāh, the Exalted, said:

﴿ قُلْ أُوحِيَ إِلَيَّ أَنَّهُ اسْتَمَعَ نَفَرٌ مِّنَ الْجِنِّ فَقَالُوا إِنَّا سَمِعْنَا قُرْآنًا عَجَبًا ﴾

Say, [O Muḥammad], "It has been revealed to me that a group of the *jinn* listened and said, 'Indeed, we have heard an amazing Qur'an.'"[2]

"Distancing those who are deaf," meaning it distances those who turn a deaf ear to listening to its guidance and the truth, which the Book of Allāh ﷻ has come with.

[1] Sūrah al-Ḥashr, 59:21

[2] Sūrah al-Jinn, 72:1

The Jinn Who Heard the Qur'an from the Prophet

Poem

لَمْ تَلْبَثِ الْجِنُّ إِذْ أَصْغَتْ لِتَسْمَعَهُ إِنْ بادَرُوا نُذُرًا مِنْهم لِقَوْمِهِمِ

The *jinn* did not linger when they tilted in to listen, before rushing to warn their people.

Explanation

Here it mentions the story of a group of *jinn* whom Allāh ﷻ honored, and they listened to the Qur'an from the voice of the Prophet ﷺ.

"They tilted in," meaning to bend or lean over, and incline toward something. As Allāh, the Exalted, said:

﴿ وَلِتَصْغَىٰٓ إِلَيْهِ أَفْـِٔدَةُ ٱلَّذِينَ لَا يُؤْمِنُونَ بِٱلْـَٔاخِرَةِ ﴿١١٣﴾ ﴾

And [it is] so the hearts of those who disbelieve in the Hereafter will incline toward it.[1]

[1] Sūrah al-'An'ām, 113

"Before rushing to warn their people," meaning once they heard this wise reminder, and this great speech, they returned to their people as warners. As Allāh, the Exalted, said:

﴿وَإِذْ صَرَفْنَا إِلَيْكَ نَفَرًا مِّنَ الْجِنِّ يَسْتَمِعُونَ الْقُرْآنَ فَلَمَّا حَضَرُوهُ قَالُوا
أَنصِتُوا ۖ فَلَمَّا قُضِيَ وَلَّوْا إِلَىٰ قَوْمِهِم مُّنذِرِينَ ﴿٢٩﴾ قَالُوا يَا قَوْمَنَا إِنَّا
سَمِعْنَا كِتَابًا أُنزِلَ مِن بَعْدِ مُوسَىٰ مُصَدِّقًا لِّمَا بَيْنَ يَدَيْهِ يَهْدِي إِلَى
الْحَقِّ وَإِلَىٰ طَرِيقٍ مُّسْتَقِيمٍ ﴿٣٠﴾ يَا قَوْمَنَا أَجِيبُوا دَاعِيَ اللَّهِ وَآمِنُوا بِهِ
يَغْفِرْ لَكُم مِّن ذُنُوبِكُمْ وَيُجِرْكُم مِّنْ عَذَابٍ أَلِيمٍ ﴿٣١﴾﴾

And (remember) when We sent toward you (Muḥammad) a group of *jinn*, (quietly) listening to the Qur'an. When they stood in the presence, they said, "Listen in silence!" And when it was finished, they returned to their people, as warners. They said, "O our people, indeed we have heard a Book revealed after Mūsā, confirming what was before it, which guides to the truth and to a straight path. O our people, respond to the Messenger of Allāh and believe in him; Allāh will forgive for you your sins and protect you from a painful punishment.[1]

[1] Sūrah al-'Aḥqāf, 31

The Miracle of the Noble Qur'an

Poem

اللهُ أكْبَرُ ما قدْ حازَ مِن عِبَرٍ ومِن بَيانٍ وإعْجازٍ ومِن حِكَمِ

Allāhu Akbar, it contains lessons of clarity; and inimitability and wisdom.

Explanation

The Shaykh says the *takbīr* (Allāh is the Greatest) in this poem, and that which follows, is glorification of Allāh ﷻ. The *takbīr* is said to glorify Allāh ﷻ and due to amazement. A *takbīr* similar to this is the *takbīr* of the companions when the Prophet ﷺ gave them the glad tidings that the Muslims would be half of the inhabitants of Paradise. They responded by saying Allāhu Akbar.[1]

"It contains lessons of clarity," as Allāh, the Exalted, said:

﴿ هَٰذَا بَيَانٌ لِّلنَّاسِ ﴿١٣٨﴾ ﴾

[1] Al Bukhārī, 3348 and Muslim, 222

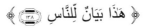

This (the Qur'an) is a clear statement for mankind.[1]

It has clear evidence that explains to the people the difference between truth and falsehood, guidance from misguidance, and disbelief from faith.

The word (إعْجاز) inimitability comes from the word that means the opposite of ability. The meaning of the inimitability of the Qur'an is the inability of the creation, and a challenge to them to bring anything comparable to the Qur'an.

Poem

والله أكبَرُ إذْ أعْيَتْ بلاغَتُهُ وحُسْنُ تَرْكِيبِهِ للعُرْبِ والعَجَمِ

Allāhu Akbar, its eloquence and its good composition
have rendered the Arab and non-Arab incapable.

Explanation

Eloquence is the linguistic correctness of the speech, and how it coincides with the required situation.

"Its eloquence and composition have rendered the Arab and non-Arab incapable," meaning the eloquence of the Qur'an and its good composition have rendered the Arab and non-Arab powerless for anyone of them to produce anything like it, or even one chapter like it.

[1] Sūrah 'Āli 'Imrān, 3:138

The Failure of Those Who Tried to Emulate the Qur'an

Poem

كَمْ مُلْحِدٍ رامَ أن يُبْدِي مُعارَضَةً فعَادَ بالذُّلِّ والْخُسْرانِ والرَّغَمِ

How many deviants sought to bring an opposition;
and returned debased, defeated and belittled.

Explanation

"Deviant"; the word (مُلْحِد) deviant is to incline away from the truth, and to introduce that which is not from it.

"How many deviants sought to bring an opposition," meaning they sought to bring something that opposes the Qur'an.

"And returned debased, defeated and belittled"; numerous deviants attempted to bring something similar to the Qur'an, and the end result was humiliation, defeat and belittlement.

History has shown that those who attempted to bring something similar to the Qur'an faced one of two outcomes. Either they were faced with failure and inability; or they produced some absurdities, nonsense or loathsome speech.

The first example is what was mentioned by as-Shawkani in his explanation of the beginning of Sūrah al-Mā'idah, "It (the Qur'an) contains eloquence which renders human ability incapable. It contains verdicts with inclusions such as fulfilling the trust, permitting camels, cattle and sheep; along with exclusion of that which is not permissible, such as prohibiting hunting within the limits of the sanctuary, and allowing what is outside the sanctuary. It has been narrated concerning a discussion among some philosophers from Canada. A group of them said to one of them, "O wise one, work with us to produce our own Qur'an." He replied, "Okay! I will work on my portion." He disappeared for a number of days and then returned. He said, "By Allāh, I am not able, and no one has the ability to do so! Verily, I opened the *muṣḥaf* and turned to Sūrah al-Mā'idah. When I opened this chapter, it spoke of fulfilling the trust and the prohibition of violating it, it allows certain matters in general, and then mentioned the exceptions; then it spoke of His power and wisdom. All of this was contained in just two lines. No one is able to produce anything similar to this."

The second example is found in the story of Musaylimah, the liar. Ibn Kathīr mentioned this story in his *tafsīr*. He said, "'Amr ibn al-'Āṣ—before he embraced Islam—went to Musaylimah, the liar. Musaylimah said to him, "What has been revealed to your companion in Mecca at this time?" 'Amr said to him, "Indeed, a concise, eloquent sūrah has been revealed to him." Musaylimah replied, "What is it?" 'Amr said:

﴿ وَالْعَصْرِ ۝١ إِنَّ الْإِنسَانَ لَفِي خُسْرٍ ۝٢ إِلَّا الَّذِينَ آمَنُوا وَعَمِلُوا الصَّالِحَاتِ وَتَوَاصَوْا بِالْحَقِّ وَتَوَاصَوْا بِالصَّبْرِ ۝٣ ﴾

By the time; indeed, mankind is in loss; except those who believe and do righteous good deeds, and recommend one another to the truth, and recommend one another to patience.[1]

Musaylimah thought for an hour or so, then he raised his head and said, "Indeed, something similar to this has been revealed to me." 'Amr said, "What is it?" Musaylimah replied:

يَا وَبْرُ يَا وَبْرُ إِنَّمَا أَنْتِ أُذُنَانِ وَصَدْرٌ، وَسَائِرُكَ حَقْرٌ فَقْرٌ

O rock rabbit, O rock rabbit, you are only two ears and a chest, and the rest of you is lowly and impoverished

Then Musaylimah said, "O 'Amr, what do you think about it?" 'Amr said, "By Allāh ﷻ, you know, that I know, that you are lying."[2]

---

[1] Sūrah al-'Aṣr, 103:1-3
[2] *Tafsīr* ibn Kathīr, 1/82

The Qur'an Challenges the Eloquent Experts of the Arabic Language

Poem

هيْهاتَ بُعْدًا لِما رامُوا وما قَصدُوا وما تَمَنَّوْا لَقَدْ بَاؤُوا بِذُلِّهِمِ

Away with those who attempted, intended, and what they wished; for you have surely failed in your humiliation.

Explanation

Those deviants who tried, attempted and struggled to produce something similar to this Qur'an, then away with them and their attempt. This means that this incomprehensible attempt by them has no way to be achieved.

Poem

خابَتْ أمانِيهِمْ شاهَتْ وُجُوهُهُمُ زَاغَتْ قُلوبُهُمُ عنْ هَدْيِهِ القِيَمِ

Their wishes have failed; may their faces be disfigured, and hearts turned away from its precious guidance.

Explanation

"Their wishes have failed," meaning they have been met with failure, loss, humiliation, and the inability to fulfill their intent.

"May their faces be disfigured," this is a supplication against these deviants that Allāh ﷻ disfigure their faces, meaning make their faces ugly. When the Prophet ﷺ threw small rocks at the pagans during the Battle of Ḥunayn, he said:

شَاهَتِ الْوُجُوهُ

May their faces be disfigured.[1]

And thus, Allāh ﷻ defeated the pagans.

Poem

كَمْ قَدْ تَحدَّى قريشًا في القديمِ وهُمْ أهلُ البلاغةِ بينَ الخَلْقِ كُلِّهِمِ

How many challenges went out to the Quraysh while they are the most eloquent of all the creation?

Explanation

Allāh ﷻ challenged them in many places in the Qur'an. The tribe of Quraysh were the most eloquent people of all the creation, and the world recognizes them for this trait; yet the end result of their attempt was failure. Ibn Kathīr mentioned the miracles of the prophets and said, "And likewise, Muḥammad ﷺ was sent to a people during a time of eloquence and poets. Thus, Allāh ﷻ sent him with a Book from Allāh, the Exalted,

[1] Ṣaḥīḥ Muslim, 1777

the like of which if mankind and *jinn* got together to produce something similar to it, they could not do so; nor could they produce even ten chapters like it, nor could they ever produce even one chapter like it even if they assisted one another. This is only because the speech of the Lord ﷻ will never resemble the speech of the creation.[1]

[1] *Tafsīr* ibn Kathīr, 1/448

Jinn and Man Can Never Produce Anything Similar to the Qur'an

Poem

بِمِثْلِهِ وبِعَشْرٍ ثمَّ واحدةٍ فلَمْ يَرُومُوهُ إِذْ ذا الأمرُ لَمْ يُرَمِ

The like of ten, then one; but they were not able because this is impossible.

Explanation

"The like of," meaning Allāh ﷻ challenged them to produce something similar to the Qur'an.

"Ten," meaning then the challenge was reduced to ten chapters from the Qur'an.

"One," meaning then the challenge was reduced to just one chapter from the Qur'an.

"But they were not able because this is impossible," meaning no one is able to achieve this goal. As for the challenge to produce something similar to the Qur'an, Allāh, the Exalted, said:

﴿ قُل لَّئِنِ اجْتَمَعَتِ الْإِنسُ وَالْجِنُّ عَلَىٰ أَن يَأْتُوا بِمِثْلِ هَٰذَا الْقُرْآنِ لَا يَأْتُونَ بِمِثْلِهِ وَلَوْ كَانَ بَعْضُهُمْ لِبَعْضٍ ظَهِيرًا ﴿٨٨﴾ ﴾

Say: "If mankind and the *jinn* were together to produce the like of this Qur'an, they could not produce the like thereof, even if they helped one another."[1]

As for the challenge to produce ten chapters similar to it, Allāh, the Exalted, said:

﴿ أَمْ يَقُولُونَ افْتَرَاهُ ۖ قُلْ فَأْتُوا بِعَشْرِ سُوَرٍ مِّثْلِهِ مُفْتَرَيَاتٍ وَادْعُوا مَنِ اسْتَطَعْتُم مِّن دُونِ اللَّهِ إِن كُنتُمْ صَادِقِينَ ﴿١٣﴾ ﴾

Or they say, "He (Prophet Muḥammad) forged it (the Qur'an)." Say: "Bring you then ten forged Surah (chapters) like unto it, and call whomsoever you can, other than Allāh (to your help), if you speak the truth!"[2]

As for the challenge to produce one chapter similar to it, Allāh, the Exalted, said:

﴿ وَإِن كُنتُمْ فِي رَيْبٍ مِّمَّا نَزَّلْنَا عَلَىٰ عَبْدِنَا فَأْتُوا بِسُورَةٍ مِّن مِّثْلِهِ وَادْعُوا شُهَدَاءَكُم مِّن دُونِ اللَّهِ إِن كُنتُمْ صَادِقِينَ ﴿٢٣﴾ ﴾

And if you are in doubt concerning that which We have sent down (the Qur'an) to Our slave, then

---

[1] Sūrah al-'Isrā', 17:88

[2] Sūrah Hūd, 11:13

produce a chapter of the like thereof and call your supporters besides Allāh, if you are truthful.[1]

And Allāh, the Exalted, said:

﴿ أَمْ يَقُولُونَ افْتَرَاهُ ۖ قُلْ فَأْتُوا بِسُورَةٍ مِّثْلِهِ وَادْعُوا مَنِ اسْتَطَعْتُم مِّن دُونِ اللَّهِ إِن كُنتُمْ صَادِقِينَ ﴿٣٨﴾ ﴾

Or do they say: "He (Muḥammad) has forged it?" Say: "Bring then a chapter like it, and call upon whomsoever you can, besides Allāh, if you are truthful!"[2]

POEM

الجنُّ والإنسُ لم يأتوا لَوِ اجْتمعوا بِمِثْلِهِ ولَوِ انْضَمُّوا لِمِثْلِهِمِ

***Jinn* and man cannot produce the like of it, even if they combined and joined forces.**

EXPLANATION

This line of poetry alludes to the previously mentioned verse:

﴿ قُل لَّئِنِ اجْتَمَعَتِ الْإِنسُ وَالْجِنُّ عَلَىٰ أَن يَأْتُوا بِمِثْلِ هَٰذَا الْقُرْآنِ لَا يَأْتُونَ بِمِثْلِهِ وَلَوْ كَانَ بَعْضُهُمْ لِبَعْضٍ ظَهِيرًا ﴿٨٨﴾ ﴾

Say: "If mankind and the *jinn* were together to produce the like of this Qur'an, they could not

[1] Sūrah al-Baqarah, 2:23
[2] Sūrah Yūnus, 10:38

produce the like thereof, even if they helped one another."[1]

If *jinn* and mankind—the first of them and the last of them—joined forces to produce something similar to the Qur'an, they would have no means to do so.

Poem

أنَّى وكيْفَ وربُّ العَرْشِ قائِلُهُ سبْحانَهُ جلَّ عنْ شِبْهٍ له وسَمِي

Away with them, how could they when the Lord of the throne is the One who spoke with it, and He is far above having any resemblance.

Explanation

"Away with them, how could they when the Lord of the throne is the One who spoke with it," the difference between the speech of Allāh ﷻ and the speech of the creation is like the difference between Allāh ﷻ and His creation. As we previously mentioned the statement of Ibn Kathīr, "This is only because the speech of the Lord ﷻ will never resemble the speech of the creation."

"He is far above having any resemblance," as Allāh, the Exalted, said:

﴿لَيْسَ كَمِثْلِهِ شَيْءٌ ۖ وَهُوَ السَّمِيعُ الْبَصِيرُ ﴿١١﴾﴾

[1] Sūrah al-'Isrā', 17:88

There is nothing similar to Him, and He is the All-Hearer, the All-Seer.[1]

And the Exalted said:

﴿ هَلْ تَعْلَمُ لَهُۥ سَمِيًّا ﴿٦٥﴾ ﴾

Do you know of any who is similar to Him?[2]

Meaning, do you know of any rival to Him ﷻ, or any likeness or similarity?

[1] Sūrah ash-Shūrā, 42:11
[2] Sūrah Maryam, 19:65

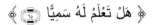

The Qur'an is the Speech of Allāh Sent Down Upon the Heart of Muḥammad

Poem

مَا كان خَلْقًا ولا فَيْضًا تَصَوَّرَهُ نَبِيُّنا لا ولا تَعبيرَ ذِي نَسَمِ

It was not created, nor composed by our Prophet, and it is not an expression possessing a soul.

Explanation

"It was not created," meaning the Qur'an is not created, rather it is the Speech of Allāh ﷻ.

"Nor composed by our Prophet ﷺ," meaning the Qur'an is not based upon something the Prophet ﷺ thought of, rather it is revelation from Allāh ﷻ.

His statement, "It was not created," is a refutation on the *Jahmiyyah.* While his statement, "nor composed by our Prophet ﷺ," is a refutation on the philosophers.

"It is not an expression possessing a soul," this is a refutation on the Ash'ari, the *Kullabiyyah* and others who say the Qur'an is an expression of the Speech of Allāh ﷻ. Thus, the Shaykh refutes all of these groups with this poetry.

Poem

بلْ قالَهُ ربُّنا قوْلا وأنْزَلَهُ وَحْيًا عَلى قلْبِهِ الْمُسْتَيْقِظِ الفَهِمِ

Rather it was spoken by our Lord as speech; and sent down as revelation upon his heart, that is awake and understanding.

Explanation

All of what these individuals say is false. The truth is that the Qur'an is the speech of our Lord ﷻ, which He spoke into reality.

"Sent down," as the Exalted said:

﴿ وَلَقَدْ أَنزَلْنَا إِلَيْكَ آيَاتٍ بَيِّنَاتٍ ﴿٩٩﴾ ﴾

And indeed, We have sent down to you manifest verses.[1]

"As revelation," as the Exalted said:

﴿ وَاتْلُ مَا أُوحِيَ إِلَيْكَ مِن كِتَابِ رَبِّكَ ﴿٢٧﴾ ﴾

And recite, (O Muḥammad), what has been revealed to you of the Book of your Lord.[2]

[1] Sūrah al-Baqarah, 2:99
[2] Sūrah al-Kahf, 18:27

"Upon his heart," meaning the heart of Muḥammad ﷺ. As the Exalted said:

﴿ وَإِنَّهُ لَتَنزِيلُ رَبِّ الْعَالَمِينَ ۝١٩٢ نَزَلَ بِهِ الرُّوحُ الْأَمِينُ ۝١٩٣ عَلَىٰ قَلْبِكَ لِتَكُونَ مِنَ الْمُنذِرِينَ ۝١٩٤ ﴾

And truly, this (the Qur'an) is a revelation from the Lord of all that exists, which the trustworthy spirit (Jibrael) has brought down upon your heart (O Muḥammad); that you may be (one) of the warners.[1]

Thus, the Qur'an came from Allāh ﷻ, and He is the One who spoke it; Jibrael ﵇ heard it from Him ﷻ, and brought it down to the noble Prophet ﷺ.

"Awake," this is because the heart of the Prophet ﷺ is awake and his heart does not sleep. The Prophet ﷺ said:

تَنَامُ عَيْنِي وَلاَ يَنَامُ قَلْبِي

My eyes sleep, but my heart does not sleep.[2]

"Understanding," this is the complete understanding Allāh ﷻ favored him with.

Ibn Taymiyyah ﵀ said in Aqīdah al-Wasitiyyah[3]:

---

[1] Sūrah ash-Shu'arā', 26:192-194
[2] Ṣaḥīḥ al-Bukhārī, 3569
[3] Aqīdah al-Wasitiyyah, Page 197 to 198

From belief in Allāh ﷻ and His books is faith that the Qur'an is the word of Allāh ﷻ, revealed and uncreated. It originated from Him and to Him it will return. And that Allāh ﷻ speaks with it in reality, and that this Qur'an, which was revealed to Muḥammad ﷺ, is the Word of Allāh ﷻ in reality, not the speech of anyone else. It is not permissible to claim it is a metaphor for the Speech of Allāh ﷻ, or an expression of it. Rather, if people read it or write it in the *muṣḥaf*, that does not exclude it from being the Speech of Allāh ﷻ in reality, for speech is only attributed in reality to whoever said it first, and not to the one who conveyed it. It is the speech of Allāh ﷻ, its letters and its meaning. The speech of Allāh is not letters without meaning or meaning without letters.

Poem

والله يَشْهَدُ والأملاكُ شاهِدَةٌ والرُّسْلُ معْ مُؤْمِنِي العُرْبَانِ والعَجَمِ

Allāh bears witness, and the angels are witnesses; and the Messengers, along with the believers, Arab and non-Arab.

Explanation

All of them bear witness that the Qur'an is the Speech of Allāh ﷻ sent down upon the heart of his Prophet ﷺ. No one rejects this except a person of deviance and misguidance, arrogantly turning away from the truth and guidance.